THE BOBBS-MERRILL STUDIES IN SOCIOLOGY

Sport and
Social
Organization

Howard L. Nixon II

THE BOBBS-MERRILL COMPANY, INC.
INDIANAPOLIS

The Bobbs-Merrill Company, Inc.
4300 West 62nd Street
Indianapolis, Indiana 46268

First Edition
First Printing—1976

Library of Congress Cataloging in Publication Data

Nixon, Howard L. 1944–
Sport and social organization.

(The Bobbs-Merrill studies in sociology series)
Bibliography: p.
1. Sports—Philosophy. I. Title.
GV706.N58   301.5'7   75–31742
ISBN 0-672-61337-9 (pbk.)

Sport and Social Organization

I would like to thank my editors, Marcello Truzzi and Gerald Marwell, for their extensive, insightful, and helpful comments on prior versions of this work. In addition, I would like to thank my wife Sara and my department chairman Frank Sampson for their constant encouragement during its preparation, and Bev Randall for her help in typing the final version.

Special thanks to Professor Hans G. Buhrmann whose figure, "Athletic Participation and Academic Achievement Linkages," appeared in volume 7 (1972) of the *International Review of Sport Sociology,* and is herein reproduced on page 40.

1 Sport and the Sociological Perspective

Every September, millions of American women suffer the loss of their husbands. Strangely, there are no special ceremonies to mark these losses and the United States Census Bureau does not issue a report on them in their annual statistics. In fact, to the outside observer, this loss may seem illusory. Nevertheless, as any American "football widow" will attest, during the weekends of the football season (and, in recent years, on Monday nights), communication with their husbands about anything except "the big game" is impossible. In a frantic effort to regain the attention of their lost spouses, American females have started taking courses in order to be more conversant on the fundamentals of football.

With a slight tendency toward hyperbole, these comments suggest the type and amount of impact sport has upon human relationships in America. Various sports in the United States and throughout the world, play an important role in the life of different societies. Observers of the American society frequently marvel at, or are mystified by, the degree of sports fanaticism exhibited in this country. A psychiatrist, Arnold Beisser (1967), has written a book aptly titled *The Madness in Sports,* about the psychological and social problems engendered by the fanaticism and excessive competitiveness of American sports. However, lest it be thought that Americans are unique in their fervor for sport, it should also be pointed out that in other nations of the world, sports like soccer, boxing, and hockey create the same excitement, dedication, and hostility—including riots, hooliganism, and international skirmishes—that many American sports contests generate for their participants and spectators.

Although sport sociology is not yet a unified discipline, my attempt is to present a coherent and integrated application of the sociological perspective to sport. In examining sport through the eyes of a sociologist, attention is drawn to the social organization of sports related activities. This social organizational focus implies an interest in the formal and informal organizational network of social statuses, norms, goals, and values which characterize sports in general. It also implies an interest in the way sports involvement defines and affects the interaction between people, their self-conceptions, and their adjustment to the roles they play inside and outside sport. In short, the social organizational perspective highlights the patterned and recurrent social aspects of the interrelationship between sport and society.

SPORT AND RELATED CONCEPTS

A systematic discussion of social aspects of sport requires at its outset a precise and clearly defined notion of sport. At this point, devoting space to defining this concept may seem an unnecessary exercise. In fact, there is a great deal more ambiguity surrounding the idea of sport than commonly recognized. For example, is baseball a sport? "Of course," you say. But how about billiards? Professional wrestling? Chess? Ping-Pong? Dog racing? If any of these activities are considered sports, then, are they sports under all conditions? To answer these questions, it is necessary to distinguish the meaning of sport from related concepts as clearly as possible.

In his classic study of the play element in culture, Johan Huizinga (1938) called man *homo ludens*—the player. It may be apparent that play and sport are somewhat related, but it is not immediately obvious how they are related and how they are distinguished. As Gregory Stone (1972: Introduction) has noted, play, sport, games, drama, entertainment, *and work* all seem, at least intuitively, to overlap in meaning. In addition, all of these notions appear to blend concretely when one visualizes a running, diving catch of a sinking line drive for the final out of a close baseball game.

Stone (1972: 2) has proposed that the mention of sport establishes the fact that play and its traditionally accepted opposite, work, have become intermeshed; for sport may be viewed as "working at play." But the idea of "working at play" is more a catchy use of words than a precise conceptual definition. Thus, Stone's discussion of sport and related concepts offered little relief from our conceptual morass, although he fully recognized the difficulty of systematically distinguishing these concepts.

John Loy and Harry Edwards have been more bold and systematic in tackling the definitional difficulties regarding the notion of sport. Loy's approach to defining sport was to build on the concepts of play and games (1969b: 56–62). He has defined a game as "any form of playful competition [between two or more opponents] whose outcome is determined by physical skill, strategy, or chance employed singly or in combination," and has considered particular sports as special types of games. Although Loy viewed a game as "playful competition," i.e., as possessing one or more elements of play, he purposely did not consider a game as a subclass of play—as have Huizinga (1938), Stone (1955), and Caillois (1961)—which (as soon will be apparent) would have logically precluded the subsumption of professional sport under his definition of sport. Nevertheless, he did want to suggest that games comprise one or more elements of play and that even the most highly organized sports contain some play characteristics. Loy considered the relationship of the following qualities of play to games and sports: (1)

voluntary nature; (2) limitations of space and time; (3) uncertain outcome; (4) unproductiveness, nonutilitarian character; (5) rules; and (6) detachment from the ordinary, real-life; a make-believe character.

In distinguishing sports from games, one must focus on the especially high salience of the physical skill factor involved. While sports obviously have chance and strategy, they are most distinctively games requiring the use of refined physical skills. As Loy has noted, even when one conceives of sports as games demanding the demonstration of developed physical skills, certain ambiguities remain. For example, how does one classify a race to the corner with friends, or tennis between husband and wife? One answer is to accept Loy's definition of sport as any highly organized game demanding physical prowess. In this context, the two examples cited would not be considered as sport, but a sponsored track meet and tennis tournament would. Loy has suggested an alternative way of conceptualizing sport by proposing that sport can be viewed as an *institutionalized* game requiring the use of developed physical skills. From this perspective, a game is seen as a unique event or contest and sport as an institutional pattern.

Edwards' (1973: 58–60) comprehensive analysis of the functioning of sport in American society has proposed that movement from play to recreation to contest, or from match to game to sport can be characterized in the following terms:

1. Activity becomes less subject to individual prerogative, with spontaneity (increasingly) diminished.
2. Formal rules, structural roles, position relationships and responsibilities within the activity assume predominance.
3. Separation from the rigors and pressures of daily life (is) less prevalent.
4. Individual liability and responsibility for the quality and character of his behavior during the course of the activity (are) heightened.
5. The relevance of the outcome of the activity and the individual's role in it extends to groups and collectivities that do not participate directly in the act.
6. Goals become diverse, complex, and more related to values emanating from outside of the context of the activity.
7. The activity consumes a greater proportion of the individual's time and attention due to the need for preparation and the degree of seriousness involved in the act.
8. The emphasis upon physical and mental extension beyond the limits of refreshment or interest in the act assumes increasing dominance.

Edwards' specific definition of sport refers to:

Activities having formally recorded histories and traditions, stressing physical exertion through competition within limits set in explicit and formal rules governing role and position relationships, and carried out by actors who represent or who are part of formally organized associations having the goal of achieving valued tangibles or intangibles through defeating opposing groups (1973: 57, 58).

On the basis of the conceptual insights provided by Edwards as well as those offered by Loy the following conception of sport has been developed for this study: *sport is institutionalized competitive activity which involves two or more opponents and stresses physical exertion by serious competitors who represent or are part of formally organized associations.* This definition implies that an activity is sport when (1) it is characterized by relatively persistent patterns of social organization; (2) it is serious competition (whose outcome is not prearranged) between two or more opponents; (3) it stresses the physical skill factor; and (4) it occurs within a formal organizational framework of teams, leagues, divisions, coaches, commissioners, sponsorship, formalized recruitment and replacement of personnel, rulebooks, and regulatory bodies (see Loy, 1969b: 63, 64; 67, 68, for a discussion of formal organizational aspects of sport). The full range of sports related values, beliefs, attitudes, and behaviors which exist within a given society can be referred to as the sport institution of that society. Numerous and diverse levels of sports activity in American society reflect the considerable complexity which can characterize this institution in modern, industrialized societies.

In presenting this conception, it must be noted that individual sports will frequently differ in the extent they embody these defining attributes. In addition, a particular sport may change with time in the way that it can be defined. Thus, in making comparisons of sports, one may find differences in (1) the degree of institutionalization of the activity, (2) the type, degree, and seriousness of structured competition, (3) the emphasis on physical prowess, and (4) the size, complexity, and formalization of the organizational framework in which sports contests occur.

SOME IMPORTANT QUALIFICATIONS

In this volume, sport will be examined in relation to a number of basic aspects of social organization: socialization, culture, social deviance, group structure, social stratification, discrimination, large-scale and commercial organization, and social change. Each major section includes a brief clarification of the key sociological concepts used, a consideration of various applications of those concepts to sport, and a review and discussion of what is known about the specific social aspects of sport.

It must be emphasized at this point, that while an effort to cover a considerable amount of the relevant literature has been made, this discussion is not meant to be an all-encompassing treatment of sport and social organization. By illustrating the applicability of the sociological perspective to sport through examples from a relatively small number of well-known American sports, the sociological concepts and assumptions are often limited in their generalizability. This focus is a function of the personal biases, interests, or expertise of the author, as well as the availability of relevant literature. The limitations of this focus must be kept in mind throughout this volume, implying that the reader cannot automatically assume that the proposed analysis can be validly applied to sports not explicitly mentioned, or to sports in other countries. In addition, sport sociology is a young discipline, and thus, there is a relative scarcity of valid and reliable sociological evidence concerning even well-known American sports, making the analysis of *these* sports highly tentative.

Hopefully, this volume will suggest a way of viewing sports that is not always made obvious by the sports section of the local newspaper, by *Sports Illustrated* magazine, or by the guy who announces the scores on the six and eleven o'clock news. This volume is not a conscious attempt to tear down or build up sport, though insofar it destroys myths, it may seem excessively critical in intent. It does not presume that an understanding and appreciation of sport's social significance must be based on detailed knowledge concerning the joys and dangers of the "Wishbone T" in football or the appropriate use of a topspin backhand in tennis. Rather, this volume is an effort to show how the sociological perspective can be applied to sport; and it is an attempt to add another dimension to our understanding of a part of social life that we often fail to look at with the seriousness it deserves.

2 Sport, Socialization, and Culture

Human society cannot persist without social order, or without pattern-ing and predictability in human relationships. Social order in the various group, institutional and societal contexts which constitute human society, is made possible by the establishment of social identities and the acqui-sition of culture through the process of socialization. A social identity is a person's conception of who he or she is in a given social setting, for example, viewing themselves as a star athlete, a mediocre coach, or a rabid fan.

Culture can be understood as the sum of the socially shared knowledge about what is and what ought to be that is symbolically transmitted from generation to generation. More specifically, a culture comprises knowledge about the skills, facilities, roles, norms, beliefs, goals, and values of a given social system. Thus, knowledge about current and past scoring, rebounding, and assist leaders; about current and past team champions; about the uniforms worn by players and the sports palaces where the games are played; about the importance of conditioning, speed, team play and the fast break, all form part of the culture of basketball.

To become a member of any social system, one must be socialized. When a person has become adequately socialized into a social system—like a team—he has developed a clear sense of who he is in that social situation. He has begun to think, feel, and act in accordance with the rules or behavioral expectations embodied in its culture. Thus, when traded from one team to another, a person does not *really* become part of the new team until he identifies himself as a member and *voluntarily* plays the role and abides by the rules established. One could say that when Duane Thomas was traded by the Dallas Cowboys to the New England Patriots, he never really became a member of his new football team because he refused to do what the Patriot coaches and management expected him to do and he could not accept their training rules. As a result of their failure to socialize him adequately, the Patriots finally returned him to Dallas. This example underscores two important points about socialization. First, social systems require that their members learn and conform to the relevant behavioral expectations embodied in the culture of the system. Second, socialization efforts aimed at producing such internalization of culture and conforming behavior are not always successful. Unsuccessful socialization implies a certain amount of disorder for a given social system.

Thus, every social system can be viewed as an agent of socialization with its own distinct set of cultural rules. The most inclusive and significant social system regarding socialization is society. There are diverse social systems within a society which are differentiated from each other by their cultural content and the specific nature of socialization experiences to which their respective members are exposed. An indication of the nature of socialization in the social systems of sport will be provided in a general discussion in the next section of the roles through which people are involved in sport. A more specific analysis in the following section will be of the dominant value themes in American sport. In the final section of this chapter, the relationship between sport and national culture will be considered.

INVOLVEMENT IN SPORT

An elaboration of the original conceptual work of Kenyon (1969a, 1969b) and its subsequent refinement by Edwards (1973: 85–86) provide a useful basis for considering the various ways people are involved in sport. The two most basic modes of involvement can be called "primary involvement" and "secondary involvement." Primary involvement refers to formally prescribed *visible or audible* participation in sports contests during the staging of competitive action or intermission activities. Obviously, this definition accounts for the fact that so many modern sports contests are "spectacular displays" (Stone, 1955).

Primary involvement may also be direct or indirect. *Direct primary involvement* is performance of the physical tasks which are essential for sports contests. The major form of direct primary involvement is the role of the athlete. *Indirect primary involvement* is participation in primary activities other than actual physical competition. As examples, indirect primary roles include: onfield team administrators (coaches, doctors, trainers); onfield game administrators (referees, scorekeepers, timekeepers); expressive leaders (cheerleaders, band members); and game commentators (public address announcers, television and radio reporters).

Secondary involvement is a residual category which encompasses all forms of participation in sport that are not primary. *Direct secondary involvement* is basically, nonpublic participation in the production or control of sports related enterprises. Major forms of direct secondary roles include: financial controllers (professional club owners, promoters, alumni, members of university and high school athletic policy committees); regulators (members of rules committees and sports governing bodies, athletic directors); peripheral entrepreneurs (sports equipment manufacturers, retailers, concessionaires); technical production staff members (grounds crews, mass media production crews); reporter analysts (sports writers, television and radio newsmen, sociologists of sport); and publicists (including public relations personnel). *Indirect secondary involvement* is participation in the consumption of sports related events, information, and goods. The main forms of consumer roles are played by people who watch in person or through television or films, listen to, or read about sports related activities, and become occasional spectators or "fans" (which, according to Edwards [1973: 86], implies that they are sports "fanatics").

One can find various examples of sports involvement in the United States, where many sports have become so highly organized. Few people are not at least periodically involved with some sport in an indirect secondary manner. In trying to understand the widespread involvement in sport in societies such as the U.S., it seems appropriate to consider the basic values and functions attributed to it. In the next section, we will examine the dominant cultural themes of American sport.

DOMINANT CULTURAL THEMES IN SPORT

Harry Edwards has conducted the most systematic investigation of the dominant value orientations in sport to date. He has surveyed statements of opinion, belief, and principle about sport in America that have appeared in newspapers, magazines, and a leading athletic journal. On the basis of his research, he has formulated a conception of "the dominant American sports creed." Edwards (1973: 63–69, Appendix A) has proposed that this "creed" be viewed as an ideology aimed at convincing people of the virtues of participation in sport. Thus, his analysis cannot only be seen as an analysis of the central values publicly accepted by people in sports related roles but, it can also be considered as an analysis of what these people have *publicly* claimed to be the *actual* benefits that result from sports involvement. In examining the dominant American sports creed, it is worth noting similarities between the claimed virtues of sport that are embodied in this creed and the dominant value orientations of American society in general.

According to Edwards, the core of this creed is represented by the following seven central themes which encompass twelve specific categories of belief:

1. Character: encompassing (a) general statements pertaining to character development and relating sports to such traits as clean living, proper grooming, "red-bloodedness," and statements specifically relating sport to the development of (b) loyalty and (c) altruism.
2. Discipline: relating sport to the development of (d) social control and self-control.
3. Competition: including statements and slogans relating sport specifically to (e) the development of fortitude and more generally to (f) preparation for life and (g) providing opportunities of advancement for the individual.
4. Physical fitness: (h) statements and slogans relating sport to the achievement of physical health.
5. Mental fitness: statements relating sports to the development of (i) mental alertness and to (j) educational achievement.
6. Religiosity: (k) expressions relating sports achievement to traditional American Christianity.
7. Nationalism: (l) statements relating sports involvement to the development of patriotism.

In examining these creedal beliefs, it is necessary to consider Edwards' empirically based contention "that the claims made on behalf of sport do not have sufficient basis in current knowledge to justify the dogmatic certainty with which they are expressed" (1973: 329). Of course, experience shows us that people often believe what they want and need, or are supposed to believe, regardless of the facts. In addition, those in institutionalized roles of authority and responsibility like to believe and have others believe, that what they are doing is what society deems to be worthwhile, good, and virtuous. Furthermore, those engaged in questionable practices resulting from intense, but normal, role strains in sport will publicly affirm their faith in one or more of the tenets of the sports creed to rationalize their behavior to themselves and to others. Hence, coaches who face strong pressures to win rationalize their dubious prodding of talented, but injured, athletes into action as character building. Edwards has contended that although success or winning is the major concern of persons involved in sport, the significance of winning remains an *implicit* part of sport's value system. It remains implicit because of the pervasive notion that close adherence to the *explicitly* articulated tenets of the sports creed will lead to the reward of victory (Edwards, 1973: 126).

The importance of winning as the primary, if not exclusive, aim of athletic participation has been discussed by numerous observers and participants such as Schafer, (1971) and Snyder, (1971). But evidence suggests that the salience of this value may be associated with the degree of organization or institutionalization of athletic activity. Harry Webb (1969a) drew some interesting conclusions about changes in children's attitudes toward play, games, and sport, on the basis of questionnaire responses from random samples of students enrolled in the third, sixth, eighth, tenth, and twelfth grades of public and parochial schools in Battle Creek, Michigan in 1967. At each grade level, Webb asked students to rank what was most important to them in playing a game: to play it as well as you can (skill), to beat your opponent (victory), or to play the game fairly (fairness). He observed that the structure of play activities became more complex and rational (i.e., more institutionalized) as they grew older, and that the children's attitudes became more "professionalized" meaning that skill was substituted for fairness as the paramount factor in play and that victory assumed increasing importance. It might be noted that as play activities become more complex and rational, they increasingly approximate the basic structural characteristics of sport (rather than play, *per se*). A fruitful extension of Webb's work to sports contexts would be to examine the extent to which professionalization of attitudes occurs in different sports and in different cultural settings.

A clearer indication that winning may be more important than how you play the game in organized athletics has been provided by Deane Richardson (1962). The results of his study suggested that a higher degree of sportsmanship is *not* necessarily an outcome of athletic involvement. While analyzing responses from 233 senior male physical education majors at fifteen institutions concerning their beliefs about sportsmanship, Richardson found that non-letter winners indicated a higher degree of sportsmanship than letter winners; students not receiving athletic grants scored much higher than respondents receiving such grants; and football players ranked below athletes in all other sports in test scores.

Receiving an athletic grant, and perhaps a letter as well, reflected a higher degree of involvement in the more complex, rational and win oriented forms of sport than not receiving a grant or a letter. Thus, it may be that the more involved one is in highly competitive forms of sport, the more likely sportsmanship will be forsaken in the pursuit of victory.

SPORT AND NATIONAL CULTURE

A good indication of the way national culture shapes the practice of sport (and the substance of socialization experiences within it) is provided by David Riesman and Reuel Denney (1951) in their article on football in America. They traced the fate of rugby football in America after it had been imported from England in the 1870s. The game was first adopted in America by members of the elite, specifically by students at Harvard and Yale. Two sets of factors

13

were proposed to explain the changes which occurred in rugby on the American continent. First, the English rules were quite ambiguous at the time rugby was adopted in America; and second, the game gradually became increasingly adapted to the distinctive American social and cultural setting.

In response to the ambiguity about the legality of deliberately taking the ball from the mass of tangled players—or scrum—and running with it, the American game of football produced the role of the center. This practice of centering the ball was followed by a number of changes which over a period of twenty-five years, resulted in the transformation of the American game from one of kicking, to one of kicking and running, to one of kicking, running, and passing. Distinctive features of American football which evolved along with the forward pass were a minimum yardage rule preventing either side from monopolizing possession of the ball; highly formalized offensive and defensive tactics, rationally planned and practiced before each game; the use of numerical signals for snapping the ball and designating specific plays; and an elaborate division of labor.

According to Riesman and Denney, one could interpret the introductions of running, the minimum yardage rule, mass play, and the forward pass as responses to the need of American spectators for constant excitement and visible action. The emergence of clear, standardized, formal rules could be seen as a result of the increasing diversity of the social backgrounds of participants in football. This expansion of participation, which was consistent with American democratic ideology, demanded the formalization of the rules to prevent differences of opinion that informal collegiate, class, or local interpretations could produce. The rationalization of the game could be viewed as a partial outcome of the capitalistic emphasis on productive efficiency in American society. The general thrust of the interpretive remarks that can be extracted or inferred from Riesman and Denney's analysis is that the sports arena will accommodate itself and its culture to the rules and themes embodied in the broader culture of the society. In particular, the culture of sport and the process of sports socialization bear some important similarities to the patterns of culture and socialization in the broader societal context.

Additional support for this conclusion is provided by Louis Zurcher and Arnold Meadow (1972: 193), who have argued that institutionalized and nationally popular sport and the family are interrelated, and that both reflect national cultural themes and display similar patterns of socialization. Zurcher and Meadow have attempted to substantiate their argument by contrasting the patterns of culture and socialization and the resultant character structures of the American and Mexican peoples, along with their respectively different national sports. According to these authors, the Mexican family and the national sport of the bullfight mutually reflect the cultural centrality of death, dominance, personal relationships, respect, fear, and hatred for authority, and the defense systems of the passive-aggressive character structure. They also attempted to show that in American society the national

14

sport of baseball and the family mutually reflect the cultural centrality of equality, impersonality, and the defense mechanism of intellectualization.

It is interesting to observe that both the bullfight and baseball have undergone changes in recent years. The brutality of the bullfight has become more limited as it has become less condoned. Zurcher and Meadow have explained this change in the form of the Mexican national sport and in the attitudes about its violent expression as paralleling a reduced emphasis on virility (the macho complex) in the culture and authoritarianism in the Mexican family. In America, baseball has been losing popularity to football, which may have resulted from the need in American society for less abstract expressions of hostility in spectator sports. Zurcher and Meadow have pointed out from the perspective of social control that, "baseball masterfully mutes aggression behind its reciprocity, rules, records, and rituals" (1972: 193).

It seems appropriate to conclude this discussion of sport, society, and culture with a consideration of the following remark made by football coach Jim Sweeney of Washington State University: "To me, football and athletics are a fortress that has held the wall against radical elements. I look for them to continue to play that same role" (cited in Hoch, 1972: 4). The validity of this assertion undoubtedly would not be seriously challenged either by fellow defenders of sport or by such staunch critics as Edwards (1969), Scott (1971a), or Hoch (1972). However, as Schafer (1971: 21) has pointed out, whether one views this assumed conservative role of sport—in generating loyalty to, support for, and assimilation into established society—as good or bad, depends on how one evaluates the *status quo.*

Those who support organized athletics in America—like Jim Sweeney— see the presumed consequence of acceptance of the *status quo* as a *positive* function of involvement in sport; for they believe in both the sports establishment and the established society. Those who are critical of highly institutionalized sport—like Edwards, Scott, and Hoch—attack it precisely because it encourages acceptance of goals, values, and roles they find objectionable, and rejection of the social changes they consider essential. It should not be difficult to understand why those who defend sport also support the established structure of society, or why those who attack sport are similarly critical of the society of which it is a part. If Edwards' analysis of the American sports creed is correct, socialization to the various roles in American sport, especially primary ones, reinforces the established structure and dominant value orientations of American society as a whole. An interesting question for future research could be whether the assumed tendency for sports socialization to reinforce the structure and culture of a wider society is the general pattern occurring in different societies other than the United States. This must be viewed of course, in terms of the influence of sport upon national societies and cultures, as well as by the distinctive structural arrangements and the cultural themes of given societies which shape the development of the particular sports activities within the respective national boundaries.

3 Sport and Social Deviance

Social deviance is a reflection of the fact that socialization can be unsuccessful; for deviance represents a departure in belief or behavior from cultural rules that are supposed to be internalized during the socialization process. Authority figures—like coaches—view the deviant behavior *of others* as disruptive or threatening; and they generally treat people engaged in such behavior as misguided, sick, dangerous, or degenerate; and feel some form of punishment, or perhaps, rehabilitation is needed. This conception of deviant behavior is understandable when one recognizes that persons in positions of authority are expected to maintain order in the social situations for which they are responsible.

Extreme or common deviance may indeed undermine the normative structure authorities are supposed to protect and preserve. In examining deviance and attempting to determine its meaning and consequences in a social system, it must be recognized that there are both official, publicly espoused norms and informal norms which arise spontaneously in social interaction, and the informal norms may be inconsistent with each other. In some cases, authorities may be more interested in seeing certain people conform to deviant informal norms than to official rules. For example, it may be commonly accepted among offensive linemen in a particular football league to hold the charging defensive players, especially on pass plays, whenever they think they can avoid being caught by the referees. This practice could become patterned despite its deviance from the official rules of the game. Significantly, this form of behavior would not be considered deviant with respect to the informal code of offensive linemen; and it may be implicitly or even explicitly encouraged by authority figures like coaches, who are *supposed* to be concerned with upholding the official normative structure of the sport. This example implies that in studying deviance, one must always ask what norms or whose norms are being violated.

Social deviance and its consequences are not always intentional. People sometimes disobey rules because they have misinterpreted them, or because the rules are ambiguous or conflict with other legitimate ones. Or, they may simply be unaware that the rules exist. The consequences of deviance can also be beneficial for the social system in such useful innovations as the goalie's mask in hockey, the jump shot in basketball, and the forward pass in football. These were widely perceived as strange or deviant when they first appeared, but once institutionalized, they were treated as normal. Deviance is beneficial in that it can draw group members together when the deviance is perceived as a common threat to the group's effectiveness or solidarity, as in the case of a star athlete who draws the common antagonism of his teammates for playing too selfishly or for failing to exert his full effort. In addition, social deviance may be beneficial in the sense that it can help clarify the boundaries for proper conduct when people are reprimanded or punished publicly for their alleged misconduct, as in the case of the baseball pitcher who receives a formal warning from an umpire for "throwing at" opposing batters. Finally, there are forms of deviant behavior that are beneficial and detrimental within a given social system. For example, helmet wearers in professional hockey today violate an informal norm maintained by the players. This deviance may diminish the respect received from fellow players and fans, even though the helmet also lessens the danger of serious head injuries.

THE EMPHASIS UPON CONFORMITY IN AMERICAN SPORT

Whatever the consequences, social deviance is frequently related to some form of social change. Since this change occurs in a context dominated by a conservative impulse (Edwards, 1973: 91-92), it often leads sports authorities to deal harshly with those they deem deviant. Thus, in sport, or at least in those sports which are highly organized in the United States, there has been a strong emphasis on conformity and very little tolerance for those who act in defiance of the rules—official or unofficial—accepted by authoritative figures like coaches.

To those who have systematically observed the culture and practices in big-time amateur and professional football and basketball in the United States, the great importance attributed to unquestioning obedience or docile conformity has been quite evident. In his study of locker room slogans, Snyder (1971) uncovered four which seem to capture the essence of the conventional view: (1) "It's best to remain silent and to be thought a fool than to open one's mouth and remove all doubt"; (2) "Live by the code or get out"; (3) "The way you live is the way you play"; and (4) "Good behavior reflects team behavior".

These slogans are consistent with Gary Shaw's experiences as a University of Texas football player:

> Our coaches would tell us about the necessity for self-discipline, but what they really meant was obedience . . . [The] threat of punishment rein-forced our total dedication and tacitly demanded that we should never question our coaches' authority. Like good soldiers, our job was to follow orders, not think about them (1972: 63, 79).

Accounts of the careers of Jim Bouton (1970) in major league baseball, Chip Oliver (1971) and Dave Meggyesy (1970) in pro-football; Bill Russell (1966) and Connie Hawkins (Wolf, 1972) in pro-basketball indicate that coaches in professional sport can be as concerned as coaches in high school and college sport with maintaining strict conformity inside and outside the sports arena.

Edwards has proposed in his discussion of the American sports creed that the value of discipline is one of its core components. The concern for discipline is to teach athletes a strong respect for self-discipline and the necessity of social control and that advocacy of relaxation of discipline in sport could have serious negative consequences for American society as a whole. Edwards cites the following response from a high school principal concerning Dave Meggyesy's remark that he left professional football because of the "dehumanizing discipline" enforced by coaches and the "regimented" character of the game itself:

> Mr. Meggyesy's ideas about running a team is [sic] a wonderful example of the revolutionaries' attempt to break down the basic foundations upon which this society is founded. If you are competing in sport, you have structure, line of authority, and someone making critical decisions . . . Hard work, compromise, sacrifice . . . are fundamental to this society and . . . in athletics but not to the "namby-pamby" type of life Mr. Meggyesy sees for us all (1973: 116).

The belief that sport teaches discipline *and* builds character has led many defenders to contend that sports participation reduces the likelihood of deviant experiences outside sport. For example, Ralph Schneider, president of the Philadelphia Men's Coaches Association has asserted: "We know that we help keep boys out of gangs. We have proved we are effective in fighting vandalism, violence, and drug use. The best lesson to be learned from sports is self-discipline in the social arena" (cited in Fimrite, 1971: 22). In fact, Walter Schafer (1969) has conducted an empirical investigation of the relationship between participation in interscholastic athletics and delinquency and has found that athletes have lower delinquency rates than nonathletes. Schafer, with Michael Armer (1968, 1972) found that dropout rates were lower for those who participated in athletics than the rates for those who did not participate. However, as they have cautioned, rather than deterring deviance, sport may attract conforming types and select out those most likely to become deviant. Keep in mind this warning throughout the discussion of sport and social deviance.

If winning is the primary goal of those engaged in organized American sports, and if success usually requires coordinated team effort from physically well-conditioned athletes, then there may be a valid justification for strict obedience from athletes in their behavior within the athletic arena. There appears to be less rational justification for absolute control in sports that are more individually oriented, like track and field, wrestling, or swimming. Nevertheless, a very limited tolerance of individuality among sports participants is found here, as well as in matters having little or no relevance to sports role performance.

The work of John Underwood (1969) concerning "the desperate coach;" of Harry Edwards (1969) concerning "the revolt of the black athlete;" and of Jack Scott (1971a) concerning "the athletic revolution" in intercollegiate sport, offered much insight into the kinds and scope of control demanded by

18

coaches over the lives of those subject to their authority. The hair grooming practices, clothing styles, bedtimes, study habits, dating habits (especially interracial ones), and political pronouncements of athletes have all been targets of regulatory efforts. The arsenal of formal and informal sanctions used by authorities at all levels of sport to deal with "troublemakers" is extensive and potent. In amateur sport, ostensible recalcitrance can be punished by benching, suspension, social ostracism, and ultimately, removal from the team and withdrawal of scholarship aid. In professional sport, nonconforming behavior can be dealt with by using similar techniques, along with fines, trips to minor leagues or to inferior teams, salary cuts, unconditional releases, and most drastically, blacklisting. The difficulties experienced by pro-football players Bernie Parrish, Walter Beach, Johnny Sample, Steve Wright, and Duane Thomas; by major league baseball players Jim Bouton, Jim Brosnan, Clete Boyer, and Joe Torre; and by innumerable other athletes in professional and amateur sports, apparently for asserting their individuality or for challenging authority, *suggest* that sports officials and coaches are willing to use such sanctions in as harsh a manner as necessary to suppress deviance.

Because coaches have often exercised nearly totalitarian, authoritarian control over the lives of their athletes, they have often had to contend with intense and widespread challenges to their authority. Until recently, though, coaches in highly organized American sports have seldom faced serious threats from their athletes. Either socialization has been very effective or these sports have attracted compliant personalities, but until the past few years little has been done about breaking out of the rigid mold cast by coaches for behavior, beliefs, and appearances inside and outside the sports arena. While sport has always had its colorful, flamboyant athletes, Gary Shaw's (1972: 64) description of fellow football players at the University of Texas seems an apt characterization of most athletes involved in American sport over the last few decades: "My teammates on the whole were the most docile people I've ever known. Most had seemed to accept the fact that coaches and other authorities were to make all their decisions." To this Leonard Shecter (1969: 112) could add: "Athletes mistrust the man who seems to be thinking differently, indeed thinking at all . . . most athletes remain . . . narrow and suspicious of change or even involvement."

From what has been said about the emphasis on conformity—and the intolerance of deviance—in sport, there emerges the distinct impression that among those involved in sport, rules are compelling simply because they exist and departures from rules, even very rigid and far ranging ones, are relatively rare. However, this is not an accurate picture; for one often finds rule breaking in sport, even institutionalized rule breaking among those in positions of authority. The remainder of this discussion of sport and social deviance will be a consideration of the major forms of deviance which characterize the realm of highly organized American sports and perhaps, of highly organized foreign sports existing in sociocultural settings similar to that of American society.

SPORT AS A SOURCE OF SOCIAL DEVIANCE

In trying to analyze the nature and functions of sport, Edwards drew heavily from the theoretical work of Sutton and his colleagues (1956) which appeared in *The American Business Creed.* Edwards' (1973: 64) central thesis was that "Persons involved with sport . . . adhere to their particular kind of ideology because of 'emotional conflicts, the anxieties and the doubts engendered by the actions which their *roles* compel them to take, and by the conflicting demands of other social roles which they must fulfill in their various communities and in the society at large . . .'' He went on to contend that in the setting of American culture and society, public adherence to the various core themes of the American sports creed helped to resolve these conflicts, alleviate anxieties, and overcome doubts. Presumably, public avowal of belief in a value like discipline can enhance one's adaptation to the demands of his sports related role and can justify what one has to do to meet those role demands effectively, including the breaking of rules.

The logic of Edwards' analysis suggests that if the strains linked to various sports roles are patterned, then the ideological reactions to such strains will also be patterned. Thus, statements like "live by the code or get out" serve as convenient and conventional, *symbolic or expressive* outlets for emotional tensions persistent role strains create. What is essential to recognize is that such statements need not be empirically validated or products of reflective thought to serve this purpose of emotional release. In this context, it is possible to understand how sports related role players, including most prominently authority figures like coaches, can talk self-righteously about the virtues of strict conformity and the importance of rules while at the same time involving themselves in illicit activities.

The matrix of patterned rules, roles, and relationships in sport can produce a variety of possible strains, each ultimately nurturing some form of deviance. These strains can result from the following structural sources: (1) inconsistencies between values, like winning at any cost, sportsmanship, and discipline; (2) inconsistencies between values and norms or role constraints, such as the importance of winning and a rule limiting the amount of pre-season practice for an athletic team; (3) gaps between the demands of specific roles and the capabilities of individuals to satisfy those demands, as in the case of a basketball center who is supposed to stop the opposing center from scoring, but is six inches shorter than his opponent; (4) inconsistencies between the demands of different roles, as in the case of the conflicting demands emanating from Muhammad Ali's roles as a Black Muslim and as a prize fighter; and (5) conflicting demands built into social conceptions of the same role such as those currently confronting many coaches who are expected to be more sensitive to the individual needs of their players *and* to be big winners. In the remainder of this discussion of sport and social deviance, factors like these will be related to some widespread deviant practices associated with three basic sports roles: the coach, the athlete, and the fan.

SOCIAL STRAINS:
THE COACHING ROLE

Since the passion and expectation of victory is so all-consuming for those involved in a wide variety of American sports, the striving to win is usually the root of the strains, the tensions, and the anxieties that plague many sports role players. In most sports situations, the burden of responsibility for winning is placed fully on the shoulders of the coach, and for him the importance of winning creates the greatest strain.

The basic responsibility of the coaching role is generally thought to be decision making (Edwards, 1973: Ch. 6), encompassing a diverse range of situations and people. The coaches must select assistants; recruit, instruct, and motivate athletes; plan schedules; determine line-ups; make substitutions; call "set" plays; and even arrange the private lives of those under their authority. The typical approach of coaches to such decisions is rational calculation and practicality, because coaches are made almost totally accountable for the outcomes of athletic contests, over which they *actually* exercise only limited direct control. They have traditionally been allowed nearly absolute decision making authority, since their decisions must be made in atmospheres of considerable uncertainty. Coaches have sought to stretch their authority and exercise as much control as possible, thus, the need to win in an uncertain environment leads them to try to dominate their athletes' lives and to make the athletes feel like efficient, robot-like machinery programmed to manufacture consistent victories. This role context can also lead coaches to break rules to enhance this success.

This conception of the coaching role best applies to those involved in "big-time" college settings. For such coaches, recruitment is a particularly important, and difficult, part of their jobs. In order for these coaches to win—and keep their jobs—they must recruit the best athletes possible. Obviously, the better the apparent ability of an athlete, the more intense the competition to recruit him. Thus, college coaches often become involved in bidding wars for the services of the most talented prospects. One inducement leads to another, then another—each subsequent one more attractive, and quite possibly, more unethical or illegal than the last. Since the fortunes of college basketball teams can be affected by the addition of one or two highly skilled players, recruitment of high school basketball stars, especially tall ones, can be more intense than recruitment in any other sport.

Dave Wolf's (1972) account of the recruitment of Connie Hawkins offers some especially good insights into the process. Despite the fact that Hawkins' slum education enabled him to achieve only an elementary school reading level by his senior year in high school, 250 colleges sent him letters of inquiry; one dozen flew him to their campuses; and more than fifty sent recruiters to make direct sales pitches in Connie's home environment. He was taken to dinner at fine restaurants; given money or basketball tickets; was told by some that he would be paid to enroll. Others promised him free clothing, plane trips, and a salary. Needless to say, such inducements were clear violations of the National Collegiate Athletic Association (NCAA) recruiting rules. Connie Hawkins was unable to recall a recruiter *ever* having asked about his academic interests or career plans.

Connie Hawkins' collegiate basketball career ended shortly after it began when his name was linked (unjustifiably, according to Wolf) to the basketball gambling scandal of the early 1960s. The coaches and other athletic officials who had sought him so zealously and had promised him so much when he was a highly regarded scholastic basketball star suddenly expressed dissatisfaction with his academic performance, about which they had always been aware. And according to Wolf (1972: 89), he was pressured by his former Iowa coaches into lying—*in writing*—to absolve the school of any possible guilt for irregularities concerning recruitment and financial support.

Dave Wolf's comments about the treatment of Connie Hawkins during recruitment and while in college indicated that the pressure to win is a patterned one which produces widespread rule breaking by coaches throughout big-time college sport in America. Wolf has said:

> The Iowa coaches were not evil men. Hundreds of other coaches were also after Hawkins. The Iowa people were simply acting in the only manner it is possible to act—and still survive—in the big-time profit oriented college sports system. They had to win basketball games to keep their jobs, and to win they needed kids like Connie Hawkins. To get kids like Hawkins, they had to cheat (1972: 91).

The Connie Hawkins story about the cheating and the deceitfulness of college coaches could undoubtedly be reiterated by countless other college athletes. One can be certain that the number of illegal practices uncovered and punished by the NCAA rules committee each year provides only the barest hint of the actual extent of such practices in college sport. It is important however, to emphasize Wolf's suggestion that the men who encourage these activities are not perverse personalities. From a sociological perspective, patterns of rule violations and exploitation of athletes can be explained in terms of the extreme strains, tensions, and uncertainties of the big-time coaching role.

The persistent primacy of winning for coaches has led many to break rules in a blatantly obvious fashion within the athletic arena. Basketball coaches deliberately "take" technical fouls to inspire their players. Coaches instruct their athletes to carry out certain rule infractions—as subtly as possible as normal parts of game strategies—e.g., intentional pass interference to stop an apparent touchdown in football; a deliberate trip to stop a breakaway in hockey; and calculated pushing and shoving to stop a troublesome opponent in basketball. Even though these violations of the rules produce anger and frustration from players and coaches who have been cheated and who have had penalties called against them by game officials, they have been taken for granted as normal, indeed almost legitimate responses to difficult competitive circumstances. The degree of acceptance of these occurrences of rule breaking is indicated by the open discussion of such tactics as appropriate game strategies, and the degree of seriousness is indicated by the relatively mild sanctions applied.

Sociologists have referred to these mild and rather conventional forms of rule breaking as "normal fakery" to distinguish them from the more illegitimate forms that are not *openly* accepted or condoned. The latter are called "deviant cheating" (Cady, 1972). Obviously, the distinction between normal fakery and deviant cheating is often difficult to determine. However, the recruiting violations and unethical treatment of athletes as students and as individuals mentioned earlier seem to be clear cases of deviant cheating *if* this behavior is examined with respect to the *official* normative structure of college sport.

The association of deviance with role strains can be generalized from college coaches to sports related roles of other types at various levels of sport involving the exercise of authority by people obsessed with winning. In applying Edwards' (1973) theoretical perspective, one would assume that anyone playing sports roles characterized by strain cope with possible guilt about rule breaking by publicly reaffirming their commitment to the sports creed. Presumably, public ideological assertions about themes like the value of discipline rationalize acts of deviance in symbolic terms and enable those making these statements to live with their deviance. Thus, coaches speak about the great opportunity for a college education they have provided for lower and working class athletes who, in reality, are promised things during recruitment they will never receive; are given little chance to concentrate on stimulating courses; *and* are crucial to the coach's *own* success. Moreover, coaches deny their athletes the right to express their individuality by arguing that they are building character. As noted earlier, these rationalizations need not have any basis in fact to serve the purpose of reducing role strain and tension.

SOCIAL STRAINS:
THE ATHLETE AND THE FAN

Although athletes are not directly accountable for the success of their team in the same sense as their coaches, they can still become consumed by the desire to win—especially when constantly reminded of the importance of individual and team success by coaches, parents, fans, and friends and when their athletic pursuits take place in highly organized settings. This intense desire to win can be as conducive to deviant cheating as well as fakery among athletes as it is for coaches.

Normal fakery and deviant cheating are regular occurrences in a variety of settings outside sport. Politics and business readily come to mind although it should not be surprising that these practices are widespread within the sports arena as well. If there is an uncritical acceptance of the assumptions about sport that are included in the dominant American sports creed, then it should not be surprising that the incidence of social deviance in sport is more widespread than popularly believed. Since sport sociologists currently have a relatively unsystematic understanding of patterned social deviance in sport, future research in this area might fruitfully be directed toward the following questions: Does involvement in sport encourage, discourage, or have no effect upon the likelihood of engaging in various rule breakings? Do deviant acts vary for different types of sports roles and different sports? Are roles in specific sports more attractive to conforming or deviant personality types?

The use of drugs—often legal ones—has become one of the more typical and most dangerous methods by which athletes have tried to resolve role strains created or exacerbated by the importance of winning and the demand for consistent, high-quality performance. Over long, grueling, or injury laden seasons, drug users frequently border on deviant cheating with respect to the official normative structure of sport, though it is probably not deviant when considering the contemporary American youth culture, as well as the informal norms accepted by most athletes, coaches, and trainers. Whether condoned or prohibited, there is always the possibility that naive, medically unauthorized and unwarranted drug use can lead to enduring physical harm. Drug use in sport has become widespread and has produced some undesirable effects. (See Gilbert, 1969; Bouton, 1970; Oliver, 1971; Parrish, 1971; and Scott, 1971a, 1971b.) Hal Connolly, hammer thrower and veteran of four U.S. Olympic teams, has offered this terse, but revealing, explanation of the extensive use of drugs in sport: "My experience tells me that an athlete will use any aid to improve his performance short of killing himself" (cited in Gilbert I, 1969: 70).

Athletes may use two different types of drugs—restorative and additive. Those who are incapacitated from illness, injury, pain, nervousness, gluttony, dissipation, or sloth use restorative drugs such as painkillers, tranquilizers, barbiturates, anti-inflammants, enzymes, and muscle relaxers. Additive drugs, which tend to be more controversial, are used to stimulate performance. They include most prominently, the amphetamines such as Benzedrine, Dexedrine, Dexamyl, and methamphetamine or "speed," and anabolic steroids. According to Gilbert (III, 1969: 30), "It is far from excessive to conclude that the increasing use of drugs by athletes poses a significant menace to sport, one that the athletic establishment is assiduously trying to ignore." Gilbert has advised that despite the embarrassment it might cause sports officials, drug usage is and must be treated as a serious problem. Stiff drug regulations are needed to prevent harm that can result from misused drugs. However, as Jack Scott (1971b) has pointed out, enforcement of these regulations will be very difficult as long as we live in a society where drugs are readily available and the pressure on coaches and athletes to win remains so strong.

Sports related deviant behavior that is associated with the need to win is not confined to the roles of the coach and the athlete. In a cultural context where competitive success is highly stressed, the role of the fan provides an opportunity to experience vicarious success through identification with successful teams and individuals. If the teams and players with whom one identifies are consistent winners, the role of the fan can be very gratifying. However, if they lose repeatedly, one can become very frustrated, depressed, and angry. To give vent to these tensions, fans may become involved in various sports related deviant behaviors. For example, they may harass opposing players and coaches, scream and throw things at referees, "ride" members of their own team who do not seem to be performing up to par, or hang coaches in effigy for losing records.

While harassment might hurt a player's concentration and booing may injure his pride, violent acts like throwing objects at athletes, coaches, or referees can have much more enduring effects and such acts of violent deviance can lead to serious physical injuries. Furthermore, violent acts by spectators can escalate to a point where their aggression is much greater than the aggression of players on the field in even the most violent physical contact sports, especially where the loyalties of spectators are distinguished by racial or national identities, extremely tense games or unexpected outcomes may produce ugly riots. In considering violence in sport from this perspective, Scott (1971a: 174) has lamented the "saddening regularity" of race riots following American athletic contests and the rather high frequency of mass rioting at soccer matches in South America and Europe.

According to Ian Taylor (1971, 1972), the "hooliganism" of English soccer fans can be seen as an index of their obsession with soccer. However, he has contended that more than likely it will be labeled as an index of the emergence of a serious social problem in English society. This hooliganism has included fighting in the stands; throwing stones, bottles, and beer cans at opposing players; and invasions of the playing field by spectators to "take on" athletes and referees. Taylor has proposed that the processes of changing control, professionalization, and internationalization have alienated the game from its working class fans and that this alienation has been the source of their deviant behavior. In his words:

> As structural changes in the game have threatened [the] central value [that the game is theirs] and have exposed it as an illusion, a reaction has occurred in the [working class] subculture, and in the process of reaction

other values have had to take a second place. In particular, where once the turf was sacred, now [working class fans are] prepared periodically to take up occupation of that turf in the assertion of other values (1971: 156).

Thus, soccer hooliganism can be understood as an effort by working class fans, especially those experiencing little success in their personal lives, to reassert control that has *apparently* been lost. This effort to reassert control is a reflection of the fans' sense of participation in "their" team's striving for victory.

In assessing the validity of Taylor's explanation of soccer riots, it is important to recognize that instead of being an attempt to *reassert personal control*, riots and similar forms of collective violence in soccer and other sports may be a product of a *breakdown of social control*. It is significant that Taylor was speaking about the rioting of lower and working class fans, because the values, the attitudes, and the experiences of these fans are more likely to be conducive to violent responses of frustration or dissatisfaction, *in general*, than those of middle and upper class fans. Smelser's (1962: 222–269) general theoretical work concerning forms of collective behavior (such as riots) indicates that an adequate explanation of the eruption of violent *inclinations* into violent collective *actions* must take into account the role of agencies of social control. Smelser proposed that in situations containing the seeds of "hostile outbursts," the ultimate determinant of the extent to which a hostile outburst actually develops is in the behavior of the people responsible for maintaining order.

Let us look at some of the ways in which agencies of social control *could* add to the sports related frustrations of fans and encourage their hostile outbursts. The fans' expectations for their team's performance may be inflated by team officials, coaches, local announcers, and sports writers who have unrealistically optimistic assessments of the team's chances. Thus, whatever the level of team performance, the fans' expectations are likely to remain at least partially unfulfilled. The tolerance by fans of losses and subpar performances may be further diminished by the constant emphasis from local media on the importance of winning. The implication of such an emphasis is that there is ignominy in defeat and being less than the best in the nation, the region, the state, or the county. Sports authorities also increase the frustration of fans with their team's failures through their efforts to strengthen the identification of fans with their local team.

Deviant responses by fans can also be directly encouraged by the rule breaking of coaches and players during contests and by the behavior of referees who seem biased, overly permissive, or generally incompetent. The transformation from spectator deviance to collective violence is enhanced when violence prone fans see excessive violations of the rules by opposing team members and coaches that appear to be ineffectively regulated by game officials. The emergence of collective violence among spectators is also enhanced when they have been reminded vividly and frequently through the mass media of past instances of hostility involving the opposing team. If isolated incidents of violence involving spectators seem to be handled indecisively and ineffectively by law enforcement officials then such incidents could increase in frequency and intensity, and ultimately, erupt into a large-scale collective outburst of violence. Thus, it can be theorized that the successive addition of each condition below will increase the likelihood of hostile outbursts by spectators: (1) fans' expectations for team performance are unrealistically high; (2) their attachment to "their" team is strong; (3) the contest is tense and frustrating; (4) hostile acts between opposing teams seem frequent, intense, and poorly regulated; (5) game officials seem biased, lax, or incompetent; (6) law enforcement officials seem hesitant, sparse, and ineffective; and (7) fans have been provided with salient and relevant models for violent behavior in the sports arena.

This interpretation of the emergence of collective violence among spectators is an alternative to Taylor's interpretation. Future investigations in this area might fruitfully be directed toward determining the validity of Taylor's interpretation in regard to British soccer riots and the generalizability of both the personal control and social control perspectives to various sports attracting different fans in different sociocultural settings.

Also, it may be that relationships between fans and athletes that are too intimate and where there is a sharing of values can nurture deviance in sport. A significant deviance fostered by this closeness is gambling, and a specific kind of gambling related deviance is the "fix" or "dump." While betting activities and contacts with gamblers among athletes are considered serious forms of deviance by the sports establishment, collusion between gamblers and athletes to "fix" the outcomes of games is viewed as infinitely more serious and threatening. Public disclosure of such behavior can severely damage the image of a sport, the credibility of athletic contests, and the reputations of athletes, coaches, teams, and schools.

In *The Jocks*, by Shecter (1969), the history of such illicit activities in American sport is quite long, with the first documented American "fix" scandal concerning a horse race in 1674. According to Shecter, any sport that has had a history of betting and in which the competitive outcome can be effectively *and stealthily* manipulated by key participants, has also had a history of fixes. Furthermore, he has shown that in American sports this extreme form of deviant cheating has been widespread. Many of the hanging curve balls hit for home runs in baseball, the dropped touchdown passes in football, the missed lay-ups shot in basketball, the knockouts in boxing, and the unsuccessful stretch-runs in horse racing and rowing contests have been intentional.

There are a variety of factors in sport which contribute to the role strain making athletes susceptible to the temptation of a "fix." One is the strong emphasis American society has on the value of money, combined with the recognition that sports skills can serve as a means of earning a large amount of money for only a relatively brief span of time. For athletes from a lower

Joun or
Joanies

class background, and a childhood of economic deprivation, frequent exposure to gamblers—often as friends—means greater susceptibility to the temptation of a fix than athletes with more privileged backgrounds. Additional factors likely to produce this type of deviance are a sense of unsatisfactory financial compensation for one's sports accomplishments, and exposure to cheating by coaches who implicitly and explicitly teach that a valuable end is worth pursuing by even the most illicit or unsavory means. These same factors help account for the acceptance by amateur athletes of material inducements to compete, as well as material compensation for prominently using and displaying certain commercial products like ski equipment and track shoes.

It should be evident that this cursory examination of deviance related sports role strains can produce tension and anxiety which can become quite severe for those involved in sport. By now, it should also be obvious that winning can assuage many of the social strains and psychological pressures that arise in sport. In the following discussion of sport and group behavior, the main focus will be on a few aspects of group structure which have an important bearing on a team's actual chances for competitive success.

4   Sport and Group Behavior

In the world of sports, the most basic social group is the team. Most sports involve competition between opposing teams. Even in those sports where there is competition between individual athletes as in tennis, golf, boxing, skiing, wrestling, gymnastics, and track and field, one often finds that the competitors are organized into sports teams. This sports team is a classic example of what is studied by sociologists interested in the area of small groups.

Olmsted (1959: 20–24) defined the small group as sets of people, usually ranging from two to twenty members, who are in regular contact with each other, take one another into account, and are mutually aware of their common identity. A basic aim of past studies concerning small groups in sport has been to determine the extent a variety of individual, interpersonal, and social structural factors relate to the variable of team success. In this chapter, we will focus our attention on some of the more sociologically interesting factors which have been treated in these studies—in particular, cohesiveness, group composition, and managerial stability.

COHESIVENESS AND TEAM SUCCESS

Team success research in the social sciences deals mostly with its relationship to cohesiveness. However at first glance, the findings seem to be somewhat contradictory. The research of Fiedler (1954, 1960) concerning basketball teams; McGrath (1962) concerning rifle teams; Lenk (1969) concerning Olympic rowing crews; Veit (1970) concerning soccer teams; and Landers and Luschen (1974) concerning bowling teams suggests that there is an inverse relationship between cohesiveness and team success. The studies of Myers (1962), who examined rifle teams; of Stogdill (1963), who examined football teams; of Vos, Koos, and Brinkman (1967), who examined volleyball teams; of Klein and Christiansen (1969), who examined basketball teams; and of McIntyre (1970), who examined flag football teams, seem to imply that cohesiveness and team success are positively related. Martens and Peterson (1971) investigated basketball teams and uncovered mixed results concerning the relationship of success to cohesiveness. Their hypothesis that high cohesiveness would be associated with a higher level of success than low cohesiveness was supported by evidence derived from three of the eight items they used to measure cohesiveness. Items for which significant results were produced concerned ratings of (1) value of team membership; (2) teamwork; and (3) how closely knit the team was. There were no statistically significant results for the other five measures.

In a more recent study by Melnick and Chemers (1974) of basketball teams, using four of Martens and Peterson's cohesiveness items—ratings of sense of belonging to a team, value of team membership, teamwork, and closeness of team members—the investigators failed to find statistically significant correlations between any of these cohesiveness measures and team success. Their results further complicate the interpretation of contradictions in the previously mentioned studies. However, if one temporarily puts aside Melnick and Chemers' findings and overlooks the equivocal nature of those produced by Martens and Peterson, it is possible to make some sense out of the ostensible contradictions that were first observed.

Since a wide variety of sports teams have been used to study the cohesiveness-success relationship, it seems appropriate to consider whether this relationship systematically differs for different types of teams. Landers and Luschen's (1974) research offers a response to this question in its distinction between "interacting" and "coacting" types of task oriented groups. This distinction concerns the way in which the members' task efforts are combined to achieve success. In the interacting type, group success is attained through the combination of different, specialized skills of the members in interdependent action or through what is commonly called teamwork. In the coacting type, group success is attained through the simple summation of the efforts of individual members performing similar or identical tasks. Thus, the basic distinction between these two types is the degree of interdependence of the task activities of the members and the group's division of labor. Landers and Luschen have reviewed evidence concerning interacting type groups such as basketball, football, and volleyball teams and coacting type groups like rowing and rifle teams. On the basis of that review, they advanced the following two hypotheses. For interacting type teams, a successful team performance outcome effects a greater enhancement of group cohesiveness than an unsuccessful team performance outcome. For coacting type teams, an unsuccessful team performance outcome effects a greater heightening of cohesiveness than a successful team performance outcome. Their own study of bowling teams was seen as providing support for the latter hypothesis.

Some of the previously cited findings—in particular, those of Fiedler, of Veit, and of Myers—seem to cast doubt upon the general validity of Landers and Luschen's hypotheses. In this regard, Landers and Luschen's claim that Fiedler's (1954) measures of assumed similarity of personality traits between team leaders and members are of dubious relation to the measures of cohesiveness (especially interpersonal attraction) found in most of the studies of sports groups. Furthermore, they argue—unjustifiably, it seems—that the evidence produced by McGrath and by Myers does not show a significant relationship between team success and cohesiveness.

Even if Landers and Luschen's interpretations of past results are questionable and the general validity of their hypotheses is thereby placed in doubt, their conceptual framework remains valuable. It emphasizes the need to consider possible qualifications of empirical generalizations about team success and cohesiveness and related variables in terms of the potential effects of factors like the team's task performance structure. Their work suggests that interacting type teams rely on close cooperation and a high rate interaction among members to achieve success. It also suggests that coacting type teams do not require these conditions for success and indeed, may benefit more from interpersonal *rivalries*, if the teams can stay together despite such conflicts. If these assumptions are generally valid, they help to explain some of the contradictions in the cohesiveness-team success findings.

Landers and Luschen's question about the validity of Fiedler's assumed similarity measures as measures of cohesiveness draws attention to the frequently sloppy way in which cohesiveness is used in the small groups literature. Many researchers in this area have used Festinger's (1950: 274) definition of cohesiveness as "the resultant of all the forces acting on the members to remain in the group." Since this definition is so broad, it may be seen as encompassing a wide variety of factors, all of which are unlikely to be strongly associated and some of which may not be related to team success.

A problem in interpreting cohesiveness findings arises when measures which are related differently to group success are assumed to be similar in meaning. This interpretation problem is further complicated when comparisons are made between results derived from measures of cohesiveness in different kinds of groups. When one adds to these problems a lack of clarity about whether cohesiveness has been viewed as an independent or a dependent variable with respect to group success, it becomes evident that some of the previously mentioned contradictions may not be contradictions after all. Such problems underscore the need to be mindful of the following considerations in examining cohesiveness-team success data: (1) the possible effects of the group's task performance structure and related general group structural factors; (2) precisely how cohesiveness and other basic variables are conceptually and operationally defined; and (3) whether cohesiveness and related factors are treated as independent or dependent variables with respect to group success.

TEAM SUCCESS:
SOME ADDITIONAL CONSIDERATIONS

Eitzen (1970) has pointed out the long time assumption of social scientists that group composition, or the internal variation in the characteristics of group members, will have an effect on group performance. In this tradition, Eitzen has used a Kansas high school basketball team to help him investigate the effects on team success of homogeneity with respect to certain social characteristics like social class and religion. In general, he found that team heterogeneity increases the chances of clique formation and that cliques reduce the probability of winning. (Unfortunately, Eitzen had to omit race from his study due to insufficient data. As we well know, race is sometimes very salient for clique formation [and social ostracism] in American society. And most importantly for us, American athletic teams have come to rely increasingly on the talents of black athletes for their success.)

In a study of soccer teams playing in the German Federal League, Essing (1970) examined the relationship between team line-ups and team achievement. His results confirmed the following three hypotheses: (1) constancy of line-up is positively correlated with successful performance; (2) the higher the average constant participation of players, the more successful the team; and (3) the less frequently newly acquired players are put on the field, the more successful the team. He proposed that infrequent entries of reserves and newcomers into a team's line-up provided those who play regularly with clear cut knowledge of each other's strengths and weaknesses and a ready anticipation of the moves and overall style of play of other regulars. It should also be noted, however, that a stable line-up may be a *consequence* of team success. A team may try various combinations of players until the winning combination is found and then stay with that combination until it starts to lose regularly.

Eitzen and Yetman (1972) collaborated to investigate the effects of managerial succession and longevity on the success of basketball teams. Their research was prompted by the work of Grusky (1963a, 1964) and Gamson and Scotch (1964). Using major league baseball statistics covering nearly three decades (1921–41 and 1951–58), Grusky found that the rate of administrative succession and the degree of organizational effectiveness were negatively correlated, i.e., a higher turnover rate in managers was associated with poorer team performance. After rejecting the common sense explanation that managers were fired because they were doing poorly, Grusky presented an elaborate explanation based on the assumption that managerial change is dysfunctional for the team. He proposed that managerial changes reduced morale and contributed to expectations of failure which collectively induce a deterioration in team performance. Gamson and Scotch criticized Grusky's argument, maintaining that more consistent with his results was a fairly straightforward interpretation which Grusky had rejected —that managers are fired for poor team performance and that the changing of managers improves team effectiveness. Their own study of midseason changes of baseball managers supported their general argument that managerial change has little effect on team performance.

Noting several weaknesses in Grusky's study, Eitzen and Yetman examined the records of 129 college basketball teams over a period of forty years (1930–70). Information on their past records showed there had been 657 coaching changes for these teams during the period being studied. The turnover of coaches and team success were inversely correlated (though more weakly than in Grusky's study), but this relationship was dependent upon the team's performance before the coaching change. Since coaching changes are more likely to happen after an unsuccessful season, more new coaches will be relatively successful—i.e., do better than their predecessor in his last year. However, it is also true that poor teams will do better with *or without* a coaching change. Thus, Eitzen and Yetman's major conclusion was that coaching shifts did not have much effect on team success. On the other hand, their data also suggested that length of coaching tenure may have an important effect on the team's success. The relationship between coaching longevity and success was curvilinear: the longer the coaching tenure, the greater the team success, but after a number of years (about thirteen), team effectiveness begins to decline.

5 Sport, Social Stratification, and Discrimination

Perhaps the most romantic American myth is "all men are created equal." For it is obvious that they are not and never have been. In all human societies, people are born with different mental and physical characteristics and capacities. Some are clearly "more equal than others" in such characteristics as intelligence, physical skill, and physical attractiveness. However, people are not only *born* unequal, they *become* unequal during their lifetime. A

ıman societies is patterned inequality in the distribution
h as money and the material possessions it can buy:
hletic trophies, and fame. This recurrent and patterned
led "social stratification."

ɔ structure of a stratification system as a hierarchy of
ɔdern, industrialized societies like the United States, the
ɔs, or strata, are usually referred to as social classes.
ɔ disagreement in sociology as to what a social class is
should be measured, we can define a social class in a
ɔ a stratum of people sharing approximately the same
and hence, life chances, in a society. Changes in status
ɔrson's lifetime (intragenerational) or with respect to the
ne's parents (intergenerational) are referred to as social
ɔr there to be social mobility, there must be additional
ne may ascend *or descend.*

ɔ is generally regarded as a core aspect of the American
ɔ 101) observed that "the rags to riches" myth occupies an
ɔnt place in the world of sport, for every major sport has its
recruited from humble social origins and rose to unimag-
ɔcial and economic success. In considering sport's role in
will be the major task of this chapter, we will try to determine
ɔs this myth may be, and has been, made a reality.

tent with the American sports creed to believe that the
ɔr success in sports is open to all, and that the achievement of
ɔss comes to all who work hard, obey the rules, and effectively
their (superior) ability. However, despite the prevalence of such
ɔ ... ɔort, the facts undeniably dispute its validity. For in sport, as in
the society of which it is a part, one typically finds discrimination. On the basis
of social characteristics arbitrarily evaluated as less desirable, individuals are
systematically denied access to positions in sport, especially prestigious
ones; they are systematically denied access to sports facilities, especially
high-quality ones; and they are systematically underrewarded for their
achievements in whatever roles they play.

Even the most casual study of the history of sport should provide
convincing evidence that discrimination has indeed been common. We have
seen discrimination regarding race, religion, ethnicity, class background, and
sex. Since sociologists have traditionally accorded women the same class
status as the male head of their household, discrimination against women has
not been seen as having the same relevance for social mobility as other major
forms of discrimination. Nevertheless, we will conclude this chapter with a
consideration of sex discrimination in sport, because it has been so clearly
marked and persistent and because female interest and involvement have
grown in recent years.

[handwritten margin notes: Use in Intro Paragraph "all men..."]

SOCIAL STATUS
DISTINCTIONS IN SPORT

Page (1973: 3, 25–28) has observed that in earlier periods of history, individual forms of physical recreation and sport tended to be stratified into the more prestigious elite sports and the less prestigious folk sports. The upper strata pursued the former and were able to exclude the lower class from participation, while the latter were for the rank and file. In this way, many forms of recreation and sport retained their elite sports status.

During the middle ages English commoners were legally restricted from hunting, then a very popular recreational pursuit of the nobility (McIntosh, 1971). Fencing, tennis, golf, and cricket, also remained within the special province of the high-born. Even calcio, a form of football, was restricted to the nobility of thirteenth century Italy.

Economic and practical factors have also contributed to the differential social ranking of recreational activities and sports. Participation in yachting, skiing, golf, tennis, and polo has often been prohibited to the average person due to the cost of equipment and facilities. In addition, people of average or below average financial means have not had the leisure time for extensive nonprofessional sports involvement. Playing or watching sport implies that one is diverting time and energy from productive, financially rewarding work. Obviously, the wealthy have been able to afford sports participation to a greater extent than the less privileged.

Veblen (1899) argued that because certain recreational and sports pursuits have required expenditures of great sums of money and much time away from work, they have been popular activities of the wealthy and those aspiring to such a status. With his eyes on the American upper class of the late nineteenth century, Veblen contended that a great striving for esteem or honor was present among those with sufficient wealth in order for them to escape the normal struggle for survival. Veblen proposed that people tried to display their wealth through involvement in leisure activities as conspicuously as possible. This is also the reason why the wealthy and the nouveaux riches, in particular, spend money so freely on sports teams, stables for horses, yachts, and stadium box seats. It also is apparent why they spend extensive periods of time on lavish ski, tennis, and golf excursions. For the time and money required for such ventures can be seen as reflecting on the actual or ostensible class standing of those pursuing them. In addition, they offer an opportunity for the publicity that results in the envy supposedly desired.

As Veblen has suggested, if physical recreation and sport are often pursued by the affluent to show how much time they can afford to spend away from work, then it is easy to understand why the upper class would make amateur sport its ideal. For amateur sport, in contrast to professional sport, is supposed to be play *without* pay. Extensive involvement in such activity without any visible means of outside financial support gives the impression of substantial financial means, which in turn, is assumed to enhance one's honor. On the other hand, one would expect a certain loss of respect from the need to accept economic rewards (prizes, salaries, or college scholarships) for involvement in a supposedly nonproductive, leisure activity. In fact, as McIntosh has pointed out, despite the admiration generally accorded the athlete throughout history, those of higher status in society have placed a social stigma on the athlete who has had to play for pay, or who has had to receive financial assistance in order to compete. For the upper class, taking money for play was viewed as degrading, and the professionalized sports involving such athletes were hence less appreciated. One can thus detect a distinctly aristocratic flavor in the efforts of modern Olympic officials to deny amateur standing and Olympic eligibility to any athlete who has been shown to profit financially from sports participation.

In general, the trend in modern Western societies has been toward a leveling of social status distinctions among recreational activities and sports. However, Hodges (1964: 165–168) argued that social class distinctions, in participation and in watching sports contests, are still important. Although the rigid social differences between elite and folk sports have for the most part, disappeared, still there exists a discernible status hierarchy of recreational activities and sports. For example, bowling, fishing, pool, and hunting in the 1960s were regarded as lower middle class activities. Boxing, the roller derby, and auto racing tended to draw their crowds from the blue collar class. Skiing, golf, tennis, swimming, sailing, college football and track and field appealed mainly to the middle and upper class. Interest in professional football and baseball cut across class lines.

In a study made by Loy (1969a, 1972) of 845 former University of California at Los Angeles (UCLA) athletes, it was found that athletes in contact or team sports came from lower social origins than the athletes competing in non-contact or non-team sports, with track and field an exception to this pattern. Most often, athletes from blue collar homes competed in baseball, football, track, and wrestling, while athletes from professional families most often competed in crew, tennis, and swimming. In comparing athletes who competed before World War II with those who competed afterward, Loy did not find any significant changes in the social backgrounds of athletes participating in given sports. Since the status of athletes participating in particular sports helps to determine the social ranking of those sports (along with the "intrinsic" reputability of the sports themselves and the status of their followers—see Page, 1973: 26), Loy's findings provide much insight into the existing status hierarchy in American college sport.

Other studies have shown the contemporary existence of status distinctions among sports at various levels and in different national contexts. For example, in an investigation of stratification and mobility patterns regarding organized sports clubs in West Germany, Luschen (1969) discovered four distinct social strata among the sports studied (ranked from the most prestigious to the least): (1) tennis, field hockey, and skiing; (2) rowing, "athletics" (meaning track and field), swimming, and riding; (3) gymnastics, canoeing, table tennis, apparatus gymnastics, and badminton; and (4) field handball, wrestling, weight lifting, and soccer. Luschen noted that stratum four, including most prominently soccer, could be designated as sport of the common people in West Germany; that stratum three—which corresponded to the average index score for the sports club members—could be designated as middle class sports; stratum two could be termed as upper middle class sports; and stratum one could be called elite sports. On the basis of these findings, three theses regarding the stratification of West German sports were proposed:

1. The newer a sport, the higher its social position; thus, fashionable trends in sport can clearly be seen.
2. With increasing importance of individual achievement, the social status of a sport becomes higher—which is a generalization consistent with Loy's finding.
3. The higher the social status of a sport, as determined by the class to which its participants belong, the more it is dependent upon organization into clubs.

Although research shows the persistence of social distinctions among sports in modern Western societies, it is necessary to reemphasize the tendency for such distinctions to have become less clear cut in the past few decades. Numerous investigators have observed the increasing middle class "democratization" of sport and of specific sports in societies like the United States (Page, 1973: 25-28). The increasing affluence of the average American citizen and the tremendous proliferation of public sports facilities since World War II have combined to diffuse American interest and involvement in a number of formerly exclusive sports like golf, tennis, and swimming. Speaking in general, it seems reasonable to expect that to the extent that the growth of the middle class increases homogeneity, increased affluence will bring with it diminishing class differences in involvement in recreational and sports activities. Furthermore, increased affluence will probably diminish the current tendency for class status to be associated with being a sports doer rather than a sports watcher (Hodges, 1964: 166).

Another important aspect of this democratization trend in modern sport has been the "embourgeoisement" of professional athletes (Page, 1973: 28). That is, as sports roles have become more professionalized and sports more commercialized in the twentieth century, the occupational status of athletes in the United States has increasingly approximated the respectability and affluence of other middle class occupations. In fact, active professional athletes in football, basketball, hockey, baseball, tennis, and golf tend to earn *higher* salaries than people in most upper middle class occupations outside sports in the American society.

SPORT AS A SOCIAL MOBILITY MECHANISM

The trend toward decreasing status distinctions in sport suggests that sports involvement serves as an increasingly important vehicle for the upward mobility of lower middle class athletes. To bolster our own recollections of numerous rags to riches cases in sports, Hodges (1964: 167) has contended that "college football has functioned as a highly effective status elevator for thousands of boys from blue collar ethnic backgrounds." While it seems obvious that sport has provided numerous athletes from lower and working class backgrounds with an opportunity to achieve considerable fame and fortune, it is not immediately obvious (1) how much mobility is *generally* achieved through sports involvement; (2) whether sport is a more effective status elevator than other possible avenues of mobility in society; (3) in what ways sports involvement has enhanced mobility chances; (4) which sports are the most effective status elevators; and (5) how long mobility through various sports lasts for athletes who have ended successful athletic careers. It is a difficult task to identify the social patterns which help answer these questions and despite the relatively high degree of interest in them among sport sociologists, research in this area has provided few systematic answers so far. It is assumed therefore, that existing research provides an inadequate basis for drawing firm conclusions about basic questions such as whether upward mobility is the exceptional, or typical, consequence of sports involvement in general and in specific sports.

In our discussion of sport and mobility which follows, we will consider some of the important ways sports involvement *might* serve as a vehicle for upward mobility and the extent people in sport *actually* use these possible mobility routes. A significant part of this discussion will concern the ways in which sports involvement could hinder mobility chances and the obstacles certain people, especially blacks in American sport, have faced in trying to use their athletic ability and skills as a basis for mobility.

After reviewing numerous studies related to sport and mobility, Loy (1969a: 108) concluded that there were at least four ways in which direct primary involvement in sport could facilitate upward mobility:

1. Early athletic participation could lead to the high development of selected physical skills and abilities which permit entry directly into professional sports. For example, adolescents could become boxers, jockeys, or even professional baseball players with a minimal amount of formal education.

2. Athletic participation may directly or indirectly enhance educational attainment. Participation in interscholastic athletics may foster better grades, increase the possibility of graduation, or lead to an athletic scholarship from a given college or university. Collegiate sport competition, in turn, may influence the attainment of academic degrees or the acquisition of marketable sport skills.

3. Athletic participation may lead to various forms of "occupational sponsorship" (Schafer, 1968: 3). Thus, a successful street fighter may acquire a promoter and be groomed for the Golden Gloves Tournament which in turn may lead to a professional boxing career. Or a wealthy alumnus may sponsor a college sport star through summer jobs and upon graduation give the athlete a position in his corporation. Or the successful athlete may marry into wealth by using his popularity to establish courtship relations with well-to-do coeds (Annarino, 1953).
4. Athletic participation may possibly facilitate upward mobility by the fact that sport competition may lead to the development of attitudes and behavior patterns valued in the larger occupational world. . . .

Systematic evidence regarding the third suggested mobility route of occupational sponsorship is rather limited. Thus, we will concentrate our attention on the more extensive and systematic research concerning the first, second, and fourth routes proposed by Loy.

SPORTS SUCCESS AS A DIRECT MOBILITY ROUTE

Weinberg and Arond's (1952) study of professional boxers in America, and Lever's (1972) study of professional soccer players in Brazil show how athletic participation has led directly to professional sports roles. The general conclusion of these investigations is that the social and economic gains made by athletes in these sports tend to be wiped out soon after their athletic careers are over. Weinberg and Arond showed that nearly all boxers came from lower class environments. The vast majority of them did not achieve more than local recognition and received very limited financial rewards. Among those able to attain widespread recognition and earn large sums of money, success is short lived. In general, boxers experienced a sharp decline in economic and social status after their careers ended. Thus, very few achieve permanent upward mobility as a result of boxing.

Lever found that the vast majority of the professional soccer players in Brazil are also from the lowest social class. Fame and fortune are the greatest for the players on more professionalized big city teams. But they are also more fleeting. Money is spent freely by players on the glamorous teams and positions with such teams are less secure. In addition, soccer is played throughout the year in Brazil. Playing for a bigger, professionalized club requires the kind of commitment that does not allow time to further one's education or prepare for another career. The less professionalized clubs provided their players with help to make permanent their (less lofty) climb in status. However, Lever's general conclusion—much like Weinberg and Arond's—is that upward mobility through soccer, is limited and transitory in nature.

SPORT, EDUCATION, AND SOCIAL MOBILITY

The general thrust of the investigations of Weinberg and Arond and of Lever is that upwardly mobile athletes will not be able to maintain their status gains after their sports careers have ended unless they acquire during their careers the skills, expertise, certification, values, attitudes, and behaviors necessary for occupational success in the wider society. A consideration of the second and fourth mobility routes proposed by Loy will indicate how athletic participation can help provide these tools for attaining more enduring upward mobility.

Buhrmann's (1972) longitudinal study (between 1959 and 1965) of junior high school boys in a southern Oregon city suggests that athletic participation enhanced mobility by directly or indirectly improving educational attainment. Junior high athletes significantly exceeded nonathletes in grade point average as well as in standardized achievement test scores. However, when socioeconomic backgrounds and previous scholarship (at the end of elementary school) were held constant, the relationship with grade-point was weakened—though it remained significant, and the relationship with standardized achievement test scores disappeared almost entirely.

These additional findings may seem to blunt the force of Buhrmann's finding. However, it is noteworthy that he has also discovered that controlling for prior scholarship reduces the impact of athletic participation primarily in the middle class. Athletes of low socioeconomic status still exceeded their status peers to a reasonable extent. Buhrmann suggested that athletics may be the most important means for students from less privileged backgrounds to attain social recognition and acceptance, greater academic aspirations, and better scholarship. In trying to interpret the relationship between athletic participation in the school and academic success, Buhrmann (1972: 128) proposed a model (Figure 1) of indirect linkages between these two variables.

In his study of the American adolescent student subculture, Coleman (1961) argued that participation in high school athletics diverted a student's attention from academic matters. He found that among high school students, sport was considered a more important endeavor than scholarship, and the athlete was more popular than the scholar. In spite of Coleman's apparently plausible argument to the contrary, Buhrmann's results regarding athletics and educational attainment have been replicated in several studies of high school students by Rehberg and Schafer (1968); Schafer and Armer (1968, 1972); Schafer and Rehberg (1970); and Spreitzer and Pugh (1973). Spreitzer and Pugh's work is particularly interesting in that it was a replication and extension of Rehberg and Schafer's (1968) research indicating that the positive relationship between athletic participation and educational plans after graduation could not be explained by socioeconomic status, parental academic encouragement, student grade average, or measured intelligence.

Figure 1. Athletic participation and academic achievement linkages

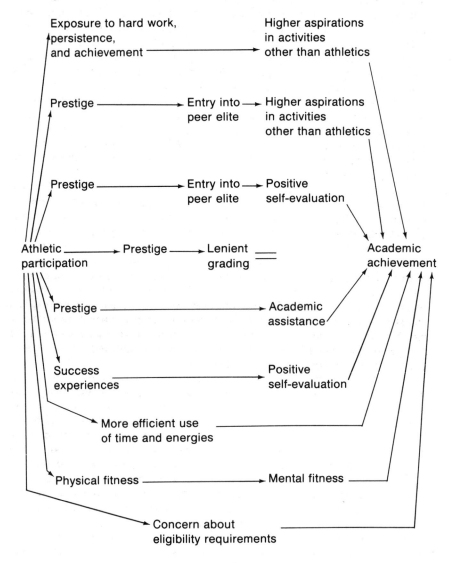

N.B. In Buhrmann's original presentation of this model, there were unbroken and broken lines linking variables. However, this distinction was not maintained here because Buhrmann did not provide a key for interpreting the precise meaning of each type of line. The "=" symbol means "equals."

Spreitzer and Pugh therefore concluded that athletic participation in high school was not detrimental to academic pursuits. More importantly, they found that athletic involvement had an especially strong impact on the college plans of boys who were otherwise unlikely to attend college.

In extending Rehberg and Schafer's study, Spreitzer and Pugh discovered that school value climate and perceived peer status were important factors which mediated between athletic participation and educational expectations. Their data supported Spady's (1970) argument that sports participation produces a high perceived peer status which creates a desire for further recognition through college attendance. They reiterated Spady's hypothesis that this process could inflate educational aspirations without encouraging students to obtain the skills needed for later academic success; but their data were inadequate for testing this assumption. They pointed out that Spady's argument concerning the mediating effects of perceived peer status applied only to high schools where athletic achievement was highly valued relative to scholarly achievement.

Paralleling Buhrmann's findings for junior high school students, Schafer and Armer (1968, 1972) found that athletic participation at the high school level was positively associated with educational achievement, as well as with educational expectations. Snyder (1969) and Bend (1968) found support for the argument that there may be long-term positive results from high school athletic participation. Snyder's results indicated a positive relationship between high school athletic involvement and occupational status five years after graduation. Bend's national data are consistent with Snyder's local ones. On the basis of Project Talent statistics, Bend found that among low status high school students, superior athletes in comparison with nonathletes had higher educational, economic, and occupational status expectations in 1960 when they were high school seniors and had achieved higher educational and occupational status five years later.

Coleman's assumptions about the detrimental effects of athletics on educational attainment seem to apply more to the colleges and universities having big-time athletic programs than to the high school level. Webb (1968a, 1968b, 1969b), in his study of former Michigan State University (MSU) athletes, reported that five years after their original class should have graduated, forty-nine percent of the team athletes and sixty percent of the individual athletes had received their degrees from MSU. These figures can be compared to the graduation rates of seventy percent for all MSU students and about seventy-five percent for all students entering college during the relevant time period (Webb, 1969b: 129). Although the graduation rate for athletes was inflated to about sixty-seven percent when Webb included dropouts with strong indications of college graduation elsewhere, his results suggested that athletes at MSU were less successful students than nonathletes. However, without controls on such factors as entering academic record and IQ, Webb's results must be viewed with caution. His findings tentatively suggest that participation in intercollegiate athletics may not have the same positive influence on educational attainment as participation in high school athletics has been shown to have. Other studies point to the same conclusion, though they too fail to consider the possible effects of academic and intellectual background characteristics.

Sage (1967) studied two groups of former high school athletic stars: one group chose to continue athletic participation in college and the other did not. The nonparticipating group, it was found, achieved better college grades, was less likely to join a fraternity, and was occupationally oriented rather than socially oriented to the college environment. One could infer from Sage's research that college athletes are less serious students than nonathletes.

College athletes who have serious intentions about studying often find that the time and energy demanded in athletic participation imposed severe limitations on their ability to study. Observations by Underwood (1969), Meggyesy (1970), Scott (1971a), and Shaw (1972), of the academic experiences of college scholarship athletes have indicated the severe strain which athletic involvement places upon academic performance for scholarship athletes in big-time programs. It appears that maintaining the minimum average required for athletic eligibility is the basic academic concern for such athletes. One would expect the typical outcomes of this orientation to be an inferior education, an extension of time needed to attain a degree or no degree at all, or perhaps ultimately, diminished prospects for career success.

It is important to recognize that in a credentials oriented, technologically advanced society like the United States, college attendance and degrees are important societal mobility levers. Athletic scholarships provide the motivation and means to attend and graduate from college with an opportunity for mobility through sport, which otherwise would not be available. This is especially true for lower and working class Americans in general and for most blacks in particular. Webb's findings indicate that lower class *white* athletes are able to take advantage of financial assistance, with sixty-four percent of these athletes receiving degrees, while fifty-two percent from upper income groups received their degrees. Although the sixty-four percent rate is lower than the overall MSU graduation rate of seventy percent, it is probably higher than the rate for nonathletes of similar social origins. The thirty-eight percent graduation rate for black MSU athletes will be discussed later in this chapter. However, it is useful to note here several questions for further research: (1) What proportion of these black athletes would have attended or graduated from college without athletic financial assistance? (2) How many alternative mobility routes existed for these athletes? and (3) How much mobility was actually achieved by those who attended college and dropped out, and by those who graduated?

Although college athletes may have difficulties taking their studies seriously and doing well at them, there is evidence that *if they graduate from college*, they will do quite well in their careers. In his study of UCLA athletes who had won at least three varsity letters, Loy (1969a: 112–117; 1972: 14–22) discovered that the majority were employed in relatively high prestige occupations. Significantly, almost half went on to earn advanced degrees.

Similar findings about the occupational success of former University of Pittsburgh lettermen have been reported by Litchfield with Cope, (1962). A comparison of the occupational status of Loy's former athletes with that of their fathers showed a relatively high degree of social mobility. Unfortunately, Loy was unable to analyze the direct effects of sports participation upon mobility because control groups of nonathletes or less successful athletes were not used for comparative purposes.

In order to achieve more definitive answers concerning the role of college athletics in enhancing social mobility, more data would be needed. In particular, we would need to know the distribution of athletes and nonathletes by social class backgrounds and the relative career success patterns of both groups. Although the empirical patterns regarding high school athletic participation are clearer than those regarding collegiate involvement, we still do not know precisely why athletes in high school are slightly superior students or why athletics provides a boost in the educational and career plans of athletes from lower class backgrounds. Spreitzer and Pugh (1973) have offered a tentative explanation in terms of the factors of perceived peer status and the value climate of a school. However, more extensive and systematic analyses of existing and future findings are necessary.

Sports participation at the college level, and perhaps even at the high school level, can develop one's sports ability and skills and gain publicity for the sports success that results from their use. Recognition of sports success can lead directly to career success outside sport, through occupational sponsorship, or inside it. In the latter case, sports success in school can lead to a job (professional athlete, coach, or sports announcer) in the occupational realm of sport.

Former high school and college athletic stars with diverse social class origins and talented athletes without much formal education can and do earn great admiration and money in professional roles in sports. However, the few cases of spectacular leaps from the ghetto to millionaire can be very misleading with respect to the pattern of career success for talented athletes. Their social and economic success may be fleeting, as in the case of boxing in America and soccer in Brazil. Even more basically, relatively few athletes are able to pursue professional or big-time amateur athletic careers. Of those who do, only a small proportion achieve more than temporary fame and fortune. In the fall of 1968, there were well over 900,000 high school football players, but less than 30,000 college football players. Since only half of the college players were receiving athletic scholarships, less than two percent of all high school football players are eventually supported in college. Of the group of college players, only a handful will ultimately sign professional contracts. Fewer still will actually play for professional teams. Hence, as Jack Scott (1971a: 179) noted, "for every 'Broadway' Joe Namath there are hundreds of sad, disillusioned men standing on the street corners and sitting in the beer halls of Pennsylvania towns such as Scranton, Beaver Falls, and Altoona." These figures undoubtedly provide a good indication of the chances for success of athletes in most collegiate and professional sports. Probably the most effective means of raising one's status through sports is the coaching profession. Loy and Sage (1972) studied the career mobility patterns of 627 American collegiate basketball and football coaches. Their data indicate that the majority were from blue collar backgrounds. It appears for those involved, that their job as coach represents a jump upward in status.

SPORT, SOCIALIZATION, AND SOCIAL MOBILITY

The last type of mobility discussed by Loy concerns the socialization effects of sports participation. It has been proposed that athletic participation may develop in individuals the personal qualities, values, and attitudes instrumental for success in the occupational world. For example, Meyer's (1951: 22) study of first line supervisors of a large utility company, showed that many more good supervisors had participated in sports activities than had the poor supervisors. Like Loy (1969a: 108), one could interpret this as implying that sports involvement develops leadership ability by teaching people how to relate effectively to one another, especially in group contexts.

Luschen's (1969) evidence concerning the mobility patterns of young sports club members in West Germany indicates that sports participation served in a limited way as a lever to facilitate the exposure of a small number of working class young people to middle class norms and values. Furthermore, Luschen argued that to the extent that stratification of a society is determined by achievement, and success is based on achievement motivation and the ability to work with others, sport will foster upward social mobility. However, his general conclusion was that sport reflected the patterns of inequality in the West German society as a whole.

Further cautions regarding the assumption that sport serves as a mobility mechanism through socialization are offered by Pooley and by Ogilvie and Tutko. Pooley's (1968) research suggested that involvement in ethnic soccer clubs by immigrants and certain minority group members may *limit* mobility chances in American society by inhibiting the assimilation of basic American values. Ogilvie and Tutko's argument is of a different nature based on their evidence concerning personality traits of athletes. They concluded that athletic competition does not mold a person's character in a way that will make him more successful in sport or in the wider society:

> The personality of the ideal athlete is not the result of any molding process, but comes out of the ruthless selection process that occurs at all levels of sport. . . . Horatio Alger success—in sport or elsewhere—comes only to those who already are mentally fit, resilient, and strong (1971: 61).

Therefore, people who succeed in sport and achieve upward mobility in or

44

through sport are unusually talented, intelligent, and persistent individuals, destined to succeed in whatever they do—with or without the influence of their sports participation. A sports role has only given them the chance to demonstrate their special capabilities.

Even if it can be assumed that sport *generally* serves as a positive mechanism of mobility, there is still much to learn before we can begin to grasp in a systematic way the full nature of the relationship between sport and social mobility. According to Loy (1969a), we need to know much more about the status hierarchy of sports in America and other nations; the differential effects of participation in sports of differing status on the mobility process; social mobility within different sports; and the extent different social and ethnic backgrounds limit or enhance entry into and success within different sports.

SPORT, SOCIAL MOBILITY, AND DISCRIMINATION

Discrimination acts in subtle ways to limit one's mobility chances. A good example is provided by Eggleston (1965), who investigated the awarding of "Blues"—or, varsity letters—at Oxford and Cambridge (called Oxbridge). Eggleston found that the well-established difference in opportunity for admission to Oxbridge between private (in American terminology) and public school students was matched by a greater likelihood for ex-private school pupils to earn Blues in cricket and rugby. It was in soccer that ex-public school students were more likely to earn their Blue. However, it is noteworthy that soccer was a much lower status sport. Earning a Blue, particularly in high status sports, conferred greater prestige upon an athlete and also provided a valuable boost to his career after graduation. Thus, awarding Blues in high status sports predominantly to students with privileged backgrounds reinforced the existing patterns of stratification in English society.

It is important to realize that the pattern of awarding Oxbridge Blues is not necessarily a reflection of *conscious* bias on the part of the selectors. The pattern resulted despite the fact that selection of Blues recipients was conducted in a highly public manner and seemed to embody genuine efforts to ensure objective evaluation of ability. The disadvantage of less privileged, ex-public school students was based mostly on (1) covert, unconscious class biases of selectors; (2) differential exposure in secondary school to the nuances of team play, communication between players, and coaching characteristic of Oxbridge; (3) differential likelihood of contact with old Blues who might inspire aspiration for a Blue; (4) differential importance of athletic competition at the secondary school level; and (5) differential ability to make the financial sacrifices required to participate consistently in sport.

The practice of awarding Blues at Oxbridge may not have been overtly discriminatory. However, it at least illustrates the subtle operation of social exclusion, class biases, and institutionalized discriminatory mechanisms to limit the mobility chances of people possessing social characteristics that have been evaluated as undesirable. In this case, the unconscious targets were Oxbridge students of less privileged socioeconomic status. Other kinds of discrimination are considerably more blatant and systematic in their occurrence and more severe in their consequences for upward mobility. Probably the clearest example in American society and sport is racial discrimination.

According to Blalock (1962), since 1947, major league baseball has offered blacks one of relatively few means of escape from blue collar occupations. He acknowledged that black players faced some discrimination and segregated living conditions but he also anticipated the continuing difficulties of blacks in obtaining coaching and managerial positions and in achieving more than "window dressing" positions in the "front office." Nevertheless, Blalock has argued that baseball appeared to be an occupational setting in which there was little or no racial discrimination. He explained this relative absence of discrimination in terms of the following: (1) the sharing of all team members in the rewards of money and prestige produced by the outstanding perform- ances of talented teammates, whatever their color; (2) the infrequent opportunities for black and white players to dominate each other on the field of play; (3) the limited dependence of individual performances on the behavior of teammates and interpersonal relationships with them; (4) the fact that job security was threatened by countless others, both black and white; and (5) the limited chance or need for blacks and whites to mix for purely "social" reasons, which in turn restricted exposure to such potentially upsetting instances as interracial dating.

Edwards (1973: 206) challenged as naive Blalock's assumption of negligi- ble discrimination in major league baseball since Jackie Robinson's entry. He tried to demonstrate how the exploitation and demeaning of black people in sport reflect the treatment of blacks in society as a whole (see Edwards, 1969). While admitting that some black athletes have achieved a great deal of financial success in professional sport, Edwards argued that the view of sport as a major vehicle for achieving upward mobility for black people is a cruel hoax. He pointed out that even if sport is one of the few avenues of success open to blacks, it is actually open to only a tiny proportion. Those who are successful athletes frequently find that they are given less publicity and pay than white athletes of comparable ability and achievement. Furthermore, according to Edwards, when the black athlete's career is finished, he must face an occupational world for which he has not received adequate training and in which he must battle racial discrimination all over again.

Even if one accepts all of Edwards' specific assertions, it is possible to question his conclusion. Admittedly, a very small segment of the black population achieves significant and permanent status gains through sport. Nevertheless, one must ask, how many other avenues of mobility directly *or* indirectly provide as much opportunity for status enhancement? The music and entertainment fields, which also rely on ability and skills learned outside formal educational channels (often inferior for blacks), come to mind—along with the civil service bureaucracy and the military. Although black people have achieved spectacular success in the music and entertainment fields, it is not clear that these and other possible mobility routes have been as effective as sport in elevating the status of black Americans. In this context, Scott (1971a: 180) has said that "it would be foolish . . . to deny that sports have not helped many black people to a more comfortable life." However, in a society where sport is a primary mobility route for an entire race of people, many unathletic black children with other abilities may believe that their only chance to succeed will be in sport. To Edwards (1969: 9), the existence of racial discrimination in college sport is reflected in the limited number of black college athletes receiving full athletic scholarships while riding the bench. He argued that second- and third-string athletic scholarships are reserved for white athletes.

Yetman and Eitzen (1971) generated evidence which *seems* to support Edwards' argument about black college athletes. They studied college basketball players to test the assumption that for positions on athletic teams, black athletes must be better than their white competitors to "make the team." Presumably, bias against blacks leaves less room for marginal black than marginal white athletes. Their data included information on almost 2500 college basketball players, of whom 700 were black. For each team studied, players were ranked according to their final scoring average for the 1969–70 season. Yetman and Eitzen found that regardless of the region, the type or the size of school, the level of intercollegiate competition, or the year in school, black basketball players were disproportionately in the starting roles. They found that blacks were disproportionately underrepresented among the second five players. To get a clearer sense of their findings, twenty-nine percent of all the members of integrated teams were black, and forty-seven percent were the leading scorers. Only seventeen percent of the number ten scorers were black, and two-thirds of all black players and forty-four percent of the white players were on the starting fives. These results were tentatively explained in terms of discriminatory recruiting practices and differential motivation by black players, for whom failure in sport is more severe than it is for whites. Yetman and Eitzen thus suggested that college basketball, as well as other sports, reflected and perpetuated the racism existing in the larger society.

However, discrimination may operate more subtly than through discriminatory recruiting practices to create the patterns which Yetman and Eitzen uncovered. These patterns may be attributable to the indirect effects of the whole set of factors which have historically determined the generally low socioeconomic status of black people. This low status has meant that college attendance and intercollegiate athletic participation by blacks have been almost completely dependent on financial aid. However, college athletic scholarships have generally been given to both black and white athletes primarily on the basis of athletic ability versus need. Hence, one is likely to find at least a rough correlation between a black or a white player's athletic ability and rank on his team and his possession of an athletic grant-in-aid. Since blacks are generally less able than whites to attend college and compete in athletics without financial aid and since financial aid for athletics is typically based mainly on ability, blacks tend to be predominant among the scholarship recipients and thus, the top players. For the same reasons, black athletes will relatively infrequently be among the lowest ranking members of college teams.

In summary, then, this interpretation of Yetman and Eitzen's main findings implies that blacks are overrepresented among the top players and underrepresented among the lowest ranking ones. Athletic scholarship recipients tend to be most highly concentrated among the top players on a team and black athletes—due to their less privileged socioeconomic backgrounds—will be more highly represented than white athletes among the scholarship recipients. If this interpretation is valid, it does not necessarily mean that discrimination in recruiting and differential motivation may not also be explanatory factors. However, a cogent explanation requires additional evidence concerning the proportion of players—black and white—of differing rank receiving athletic aid.

Loy and McElvogue (1970) tested a different hypothesis—that race in professional team sports is positively related to centrality of position. They found that only a small proportion of black athletes occupied central positions. In football, the positions of quarterback, guard, center, and linebacker were predominantly white, and blacks were most disproportionately found at the cornerback position, which is noncentral, but very difficult to play, and where mistakes are highly visible and costly. In baseball, black players were predominantly found in the outfield, which contained the most peripheral and socially isolated positions.

Loy and McElvogue also considered the social consequences of these differences for blacks in professional sports. One difference they proposed concerns the limitation of upward career mobility in professional sport for black players. In a study of baseball managers, Grusky (1963b) found that both pitchers and outfielders were underrepresented among the managerial group, while catchers and infielders were overrepresented. Thus, according to Loy and McElvogue, to the extent that black athletes are blocked from playing central positions, they are also limited in their opportunity to attain managerial positions. Loy and McElvogue further concluded that "a vicious cycle" may be operating in professional sports in America. Blacks, because they are not liked by the whites in control of organized, professional sport, are placed in peripheral positions. As a result, blacks do not have a chance for high rates of interaction with teammates and they do not receive the favorable sentiments that could derive from such interaction. Hence, the cycle repeats itself.

Loy and McElvogue's centrality explanation for positional segregation by race has been challenged by Edwards (1973: 209) who has viewed centrality as an incidental factor in the explanation of this segregation. He argued that these patterns of discrimination reflect the unwillingness of white society to share authority. In his view, this discrimination is consistent with the dominant, but usually implicit, ideological belief that control and power should be exercised by whites—for the good of sport, society, and the white members of the overwhelming white power structures of sport and society.

It is apparent that racial segregation, prejudice, and discrimination continue in professional and amateur sport in American society, and that these factors combine to limit the mobility chances of black people within and throughout sport. While these features of American sport can easily leave a strong and lasting imprint on the minds of observers, it is important not to overlook the career success which black athletes have achieved in sport, especially during the past two and one-half decades. Even formerly exclusive sports like tennis and golf now have successful black professional competitors, although a few prominent black faces certainly do not reflect a significant trend in black involvement and success. However, together with changes in other sports, they do suggest important movement in the opportunity and reward structures of sport for black athletes. Important tasks facing future investigators in this area are to identify in their full complexity the nature of the opportunity and reward structures *throughout* sport for black people, and to uncover the crucial factors determining present and future opportunities for, and obstacles to, various forms of black status enchancement in sport.

SEX DISCRIMINATION IN SPORT

It should be fairly evident that in sport, as in the rest of society, skin color has not been the sole basis for discrimination and the arbitrary limitation of mobility chances. Religious, ethnic, cultural, and class biases have also played significant roles (for example, see Mandell, 1971). Perhaps the most persistent and widespread basis for discrimination in sport, however, has been sex. Yet, until recently, sex discrimination did not receive the attention accorded other forms of discrimination. In part, this is because of the tendency to view female socioeconomic status as dependent on male status. Thus, if a female is a target of discrimination in sport, it is not interpreted in terms of her potentially blocked mobility chances, because her eventual socioeconomic status is seen as dependent on or identical to, that of her husband. The limited attention to sex discrimination in sport also stems from more general cultural attitudes and beliefs about sex and sport.

The cultures of modern Western societies have clearly specified sports as a male province. The intrusion of women is seen as frivolous, distracting, or downright annoying and female athletic programs—where they exist—are typically far inferior to those of men (Hart, 1971). But not only are women's sports facilities and organizations segregated and unequal, their rewards are much less than those earned by men who have achieved comparable levels of excellence in their class of competition.

According to Gilbert and Williamson (1973, II), the preferential treatment usually given to men in sport is justified by one or more of the following:

1. Athletics are physically bad for women; for competition may masculin-ize their appearance and adversely affect their sexual behavior.
2. Women do not play sports well enough to deserve athletic equality.
3. Women are not really interested in sports.

After presenting these arguments, Gilbert and Williamson cogently argued against each by citing relevant and contradictory medical evidence about the extensive participation and laudable accomplishments of females when they are provided with adequate facilities, encouragement, and recognition. They have stressed that reducing discrimination is not to make females equal competitors to males, but rather, it is to give females the same opportunity as males to enjoy athletics and to attain excellence among equally capable performers.

The accomplishments of a number of women in a widening variety of sports at the professional and amateur levels have gained increasing publicity in the past few years. This recognition has undoubtedly contributed to the breaking down of traditional psychological and social barriers to female sports involvement and success. In this vein, Talamini and Page (1973: 271) have contended that we now live in an age when the "unladylike" stigma of participation has almost totally disappeared in the sports realms and the opportunity and reward structures for females in sport have been steadily improving in the United States and in other countries. There has also been a growing number of females involved in physical recreation and sports. However, these apparent tendencies cannot mask the persistence of inferior opportunities and rewards gained by females. As Gilbert and Williamson have shown, sex discrimination remains a pervasive feature of the sports world. This pattern has been reinforced by the values, attitudes, self-identities, and behavior of women themselves.

Sex discrimination in sport traditionally has been accompanied by a reluctance of females to exhibit their physical prowess. In the context of modern Western cultures and societies, the demonstration of physical strength and skill through sport is not considered feminine. This seems particularly true in the United States, where the female athlete often faces an identity problem. How is she to achieve an adequate feminine image while engaged in a traditionally male pursuit? One can see that the process of socialization to sex roles tends to reinforce existing patterns of sex discrimi-nation in sport insofar as sport has been seen as an undesirable, unfeminine pursuit by females.

The research of Ogilvie and Tutko (1971) indicates that females able to overcome these psychological and social barriers, are more reserved, cool, and experimental, and more independent than male athletes. Outstanding female athletes were found to be more introverted, to have greater autonomy needs, to be more creative, and to have less need for sensitive and understanding involvement with others than their male counterparts. Ogilvie and Tutko also found far less trait variation across sports for female than male athletes—with exceptions being women's fencing, gymnastics, and parachuting. They interpreted this as implying that if a woman is going to succeed in *any* field where there is sex discrimination, she must be willing and able to stand on her own and creatively challenge anyone—male or female—who might block her path to success.

Research by Harres (1968) suggested a trend toward greater acceptance of athletic competition for women among male and female college undergraduates. However, she also found considerable variability in opinions about the desirability of female athletic involvement. There was no significant difference between the attitudes of males and females but participation in sport seemed to foster a more favorable view toward the desirability of female involvement.

These findings supported Metheny's (1970) assumption that female participants in sport were avoided—or were not allowed to engage in sports that are strenuous or involve direct physical contact. These patterns of involvement, which are in general keeping with conventional cultural expectations for female behavior in American society, were found by Metheny to be less pronounced for minority or lower status women. According to Hart, Harres, and Metheny, the most appealing sports were those with esthetic social and fashion aspects, like ice skating, diving, skiing, tennis, and swimming.

In examining sex discrimination in sport and the effects of other forms of discrimination upon mobility, it is important to recognize that these patterns are changing. The extent that they are changing and the reasons for these changes are not certain at this time. However, it appears that there are proportionately more women participating in more sports and receiving more rewards for their athletic accomplishments than ever before. And, it appears that the mobility chances of black males in and through sport have improved considerably over the past twenty-five years. It is easy to miscalculate or exaggerate these assumed trends; but it seems that patterns of racial, sex, religious, ethnic, cultural, and class discrimination are diminishing in strength in American sport.

Page (1973: 27) argued that the decline of exclusionism in sport is closely related to its professionalization. Presumably, a commercial orientation is accompanied by a greater concern with the performance skills, rather than social background characteristics, of athletes. In fact, the increasing involvement of black athletes in big-time college and professional sports over the past two and one-half decades has been paralleled by tremendous commercial growth in these sports realms. To understand why this relationship between commercial development and diminished discriminatory treatment of athletes exists, it seems useful to examine the corporate and bureaucratic nature of sports that are highly developed. In the next chapter, we will consider these features of sport by focusing on high level amateur and professional sports in American society.

6 Sport, Bureaucracy, and Big Business

The modern American sports fan can easily feel a bit overwhelmed in his effort to remain relatively well-informed about happenings in the world of sport. There are now so many sports, teams, and players to follow. It seems new professional sports franchises are born, have moved, and die in the space of months. New leagues form, old ones dissolve, mergers take place; commissioners of different sports and ruling bodies battle with each other. Owners try to manipulate commissioners and coaches and together owners, commissioners, and coaches contend with the demands of players, their agents, and their unions. Players seek higher salaries, better fringe benefits, and improved pension plans, and strike if their contract negotiations go awry and are locked out by retaliating owners. Colleges are punished by regulatory agencies for recruiting violations. College athletes are lured from campus by fat professional contracts before they have used up their eligibility and amateur athletes accept financial compensation. Few large-scale sports are unaffected by the profit motive as sports compete for lucrative television deals, and accommodate their games to the demands of the medium. Media coverage is almost year around for more and more sports as athletes are followed from preseason practice to the banquet circuit and as seasons overlap, and schedules become longer and longer.

These features of modern sport can be seen as reflections of tendencies toward increased bureaucratization and commercialization that characterize the domains of big-time amateur and professional sport. Bureaucratic organization refers to large-scale social units with highly specialized divisions of labor; elaborate hierarchies of authority; highly rationalized, formalized goal pursuits; and normative controls. Commercialization refers to the business-like pursuit of financial gain.

To some extent, bureaucratic patterns have characterized all of the sets of activities which we have so far explicitly called sports, and a commercial orientation has been a characteristic of many of these sports activities. The presence of these features should not be surprising, if one recalls that we formulated our definition of sport largely on the basis of Edwards' (1973: 58) notion that sport involves activities "carried out by actors who represent or are part of formally organized associations having the goal of achieving valued tangibles or intangibles. . . ." The specific focus of this chapter is upon the extent to which big-time sports activities at the amateur and professional levels in the United States in particular, have become bureaucratized and commercialized in recent decades.

Charles Page observed the historical evolution—which he called a "social revolution"—from informal folk contests and elite physical recreation to modern sports activities. He noted two basic aspects of this process. First, there was a continuously growing bureaucratic orientation toward "maximizing athletic 'output,' abetted by consistently improved techniques and equipment and measured by victories, record breaking, and of fundamental importance, sheer economic profit—on this count, sport has become big business with all of its familiar features" (Page, 1973: 32–33). The second basic feature of sport which has been proposed by Page is a "decreasing degree of autonomy for the athlete himself, whose onetime position as a more or less independent participant has been largely replaced by the status of skilled athletic worker under the strict discipline of coaches, managers, and in the case of the pro, the 'front office.' " He has further pointed out that this latter development was not confined to the professional domain; it also characterized collegiate and high school sports, and even the adult-run, highly organized "little leagues" of baseball and football.

Unfortunately, there has been a limited amount of systematic sociological analysis of the patterns we will be discussing in this chapter. Nevertheless, bureaucratization, commercialization, and professionalization are sociologically interesting patterns which reflect a major evolutionary trend in modern sport. An effort has been made to talk about these patterns and their effects on sport by extracting sociological meaning from a diverse assortment of relevant sociological and nonsociological writings. This reliance on limited materials implies that caution must be exercised in drawing conclusions, and that much of the ensuing discussion will be limited in depth and sociological sophistication. Hopefully these qualifications will not minimize the importance of understanding the organizational and commercial development of modern sport.

THE DECLINE OF THE AMATEUR IDEAL IN SPORT

Accounts of early Greek history suggest that the birth of professionalism in sport occurred in 594 B.C. when Solon decreed that any Athenian who was a victor in the Olympic Games should receive 500 drachmae—which was the equivalent of 100 oxen (McIntosh, 1971: 177). Later, professionalism matured to the point where sport became a full-time occupation and athletes became dependent upon these rewards for their livelihood. In Rome about 100 A.D., an organization of trainers, veterinary surgeons, grooms, jockeys, and stable police existed as complex as in horse racing today. Financial compensation could be earned from instruction and competition in fencing in Tudor England. Golf, cricket, boxing and horse racing, have all had paid performers in England since the mid-eighteenth century. In the United States, there was a burgeoning of professionalism from the inception of professional baseball in 1869. During the next twenty-five years, golf, football, bowling, basketball, and hockey were organized on a professional basis, and in 1926 tennis was professionalized. In fact, it is interesting to note that the first professional basketball league appeared in 1898, just seven years after the game had been invented. (See Furst, 1971, for a discussion of the development of American professional sport.)

As we noted previously, professional sport has not been the ideal of the high born, although gentlemen-amateurs have accepted generous payments for their success in such contests as the great amateur rowing and sculling races of nineteenth century England. Nevertheless, throughout sports history, both amateur and professional athletes have received a great deal of respect and adulation. For over 2500 years, people have been willing to provide the financial support necessary for athletes to pursue professional sports careers. However, widespread popularity and commercial success in professional sport have always depended crucially upon the general level of affluence and the availability of leisure time of potential spectators. The growth of gate receipts from spectators has been a basic determinant of the growth and success of professional sports and athletes. Thus, the current popularity and wealth of professional sports and athletes have been nurtured basically by the industrial expansion that has put more money in the pockets of potential fans and allowed them to purchase increasingly expensive tickets for more events in more sports. Industrial growth has also shortened the work week to allow adequate time to attend these numerous and diverse events, in person or through radio and television.

The growth of professionalized and commercialized sport has been accompanied by the decline of the play ethic in sports activities and to some extent, of pure amateur sports. As money has become a dominant concern of those involved, the informal, spontaneous, and voluntary qualities of these sports have diminished, and the social, economic, and practical distinctions between amateurs and professionals have become blurred. In the United States, there has not been a strong aristocratic predisposition toward limiting the commercial development of sport; professional sport has become predominant. Moreover, at the ostensibly amateur levels of college and high school, commercial considerations have increasingly influenced sports activities and athletes. The nature of the financial opportunities often available to participants in big-time college sports programs is suggested by a list of the rule violations which have led National Collegiate Athletic Association (NCAA) administrators to place schools on probation. For example, in 1972, The University of California at Berkeley was placed on probation for the following reasons (among others): (1) giving members of the football team free passes to a professional football game; (2) providing one athlete with free furnishings for his apartment; (3) furnishing an athlete with money to buy books without going through regular scholarship procedures; (4) providing a truck, free to two athletes, to transport furnishings to their apartment; (5) providing athletes with transportation costs to and from the campus to enroll for the spring; (6) lending a prospective athlete $100 for travel during the summer; (7) permitting two athletes to stay at a Berkeley hotel without cost while waiting to register for the spring quarter; (8) allowing seventeen athletes to eat at a restaurant free for periods up to twenty days while waiting to enroll; and (9) providing one athlete with about $155 cash for a month's rent on an apartment, plus payments of about $55 in cash to help with the rent on four other occasions (reported in *The New York Times*, October 26, 1972: 51). "Under-the-table" cash payments have also frequently been given to college scholarship athletes in big-time programs (Meggyesy, 1970: 86–87) and to high school athletes during the process of college athletic recruitment (Wolf, 1972: 41–51).

Even in the Olympics, amateur sports officials and athletes are affected by the pressures of professionalism and commercialism. Of course, these pressures are magnified by the existence of highly exclusive formal standards of eligibility and by seemingly arbitrary decisions to enforce them. According to the Olympic rules, to be eligible for competition, one must be an amateur of the following type: "one who participates and always has participated in sport solely for pleasure and for the physical and mental benefits he derives therefrom, and to whom participation in sport is nothing more than recreation without material gain of any kind, direct or indirect" (see McIntosh, 1971: 185–186). This conception of amateurism and Olympic eligibility should suggest the difficulty of conforming to the International Olympic Committee's (IOC) amateur ideal for all but the affluent. Furthermore, it should be recognized that in a technical sense this ideal has been violated by those athletes who have engaged in extensive training and competition subsidized by governments, universities, or businesses, or who have received direct or indirect, manifest or concealed, payments for their sports involvement.

In view of the general trends of commercialization and professionalization during recent years, moves to purge amateur athletics entirely of commercial-professional impurities reflect an aristocratic detachment from the social changes occurring in the real world of sport. Whether or not the Olympic ideals held by Olympic officials are worth preserving, it must be realized that excellence in the purer forms of amateur and Olympic sport is most easily attained by the affluent; for they can best afford extensive involvement in high-level amateur competition. In addition, the continued public acceptance and enforcement of exclusive amateur and Olympic standards by these officials perpetuate the hypocrisy endured by athletes of less privileged backgrounds who have to accept under-the-table payments to sustain their amateur athletic involvement. Thus, it is not surprising that the traditional ideal of amateurism has declined in sports settings. We have already suggested that the *desire* to earn money from sport has long been with us. However, it has only been during the past century, in countries where the fruits of industrial expansion have been reaped on a broad scale, that extensive professional organization and substantial commercial gains have been possible in sport.

THE BIG BUSINESS OF SPORT

Joseph Durso's (1971) book *The All-American Dollar: The Big Business of Sports* contains few novel observations about the unprecedented commercial boom in American professional sports. By capturing the essential flavor of the present structure of large-scale sport, he shows how extensively professional sport has grown in the past decade and how much the wallets of professional athletes have expanded during that relatively brief span of time.

Research has suggested that no single event can be specified as signifying the dawn of the modern age of highly organized, commercialized sport (see Furst, 1971: 161). Sport began to assume its present form when the economy started to recover from the depression during the 1930s and as bureaucratic administrative procedures became more firmly established. Although it is difficult to say exactly when bureaucratic administration became well-entrenched, the emergence of large-scale organization and sophisticated administrative planning occurred in American professional sport about the beginning of the 1950s. This was a time when those in control of professional sport were forced to confront the dual dilemma of decreasing attendance and the unknown impact of television. In this context, a new sports entrepreneur stepped into the picture, one with less concern for the esthetic aspects of sports and more for sound business practices and the maximization of profits. These organization persons have fundamentally transformed the character of sports during the past two and one-half decades.

Certainly, professional sports organizations have not yet expanded to the point where they pose a serious threat to General Motors. Nevertheless, sports enterprises reflect numerous features of corporate bureaucracies. For example, they must purchase equipment, rent or pay for the construction of buildings, recruit capable personnel, pay salaries, promote their product, maintain a constant source of information about rivals and possible future members of the organization, maintain an administrative hierarchy to make decisions and plan future policies, and most basically, generate revenue for future operations.

On the basis of this limited analogy, it should be clear that the organization and operation of professional sports are often quite similar to the organization and operation of conventional industrial firms. There is, however, a very important distinction between firms in sport and conventional business firms.

Until recently, the monopolistic practices of the professional sports industry have not been subject to government regulation. It is true that the collusion among sports entrepreneurs to control entry of new firms and access to athletes is no greater than the monopolistic collusion existing among other businesses *at times*. Also, despite their control of competition, sports entrepreneurs must still respond to market conditions, like other types of industrial firms. However it is *not* true that conventional industrial firms have been given the same special legal treatment with respect to tax and antitrust laws that sports like professional baseball have traditionally enjoyed.

In 1922, the Supreme Court decided that baseball was exempt from antitrust legislation because it involved "purely state affairs" outside the federal jurisdiction over interstate commerce (Rivkin, 1974: 389–390). Since that time, officials in baseball and other professional sports have used that decision to defend their special legal and economic position. However, since radio and television broadcasts have been interpreted as interstate commerce in more recent Supreme Court decisions, the immunity of those sports deriving substantial revenue from these media has been undermined. Whether or not the success of professional sport depends upon the perpetuation of monopolistic practices with respect to markets and players, increasing numbers of judges and legislators have begun to question why the financial success of the sports industry should be guaranteed any more than that of other industries. The arguments by sports magnates, even in baseball (see Andreano, 1965: 147), in defense of a privileged economic position are becoming more dubious as sports enterprises look and act more like conventional business firms.

Although amateur athletes are not supposed to be materially compensated for their performances, amateur athletic organizations often look and operate like businesses. These programs frequently require the expenditure of tremendous sums of money to pay administrators, coaches, and game officials; to recruit athletes, and cover their living and travel expenses; to purchase and maintain equipment and playing facilities; and simply to stage individual events. Of course, amateur sports spectacles also produce revenue. In addition, there are often so many players, teams, leagues, and levels of play that their administrative structures have become highly complex and formalized. The International Olympic Committee (IOC), Amateur Athletic Union (AAU), and National Collegiate Athletic Association (NCAA), all illustrate how bureaucratized amateur sports associations can become. Perhaps the individual big-time college athletic programs in the United States most clearly represent the large-scale corporate enterprise appearance which can emerge in the amateur sports realm.

The development of college sport since 1880 (see Scott, 1971a: Ch. 14) has transformed it into an increasingly spectator oriented big business operation. As columnist Leonard Koppett (1971: 70) observed, "Only in the United States do colleges and universities support large-scale, expensive varsity sports with as much emphasis on providing public entertainment as on the benefits of participation."

More than $300 million was spent on sports in 1969 by the approximately 650 member institutions of the NCAA; and more than $200 million was taken in from sources directly connected with staging sports events. The average amount spent by NCAA member schools on athletics was $548,000; but the range between the extremes was quite large. The approximately fifty schools with the largest football operations including Ohio State University, University of Notre Dame, and the University of Southern California averaged about $1.3 million in expenditures, with about $670,000 used for football. Schools with modest but vigorous football programs like the University of Delaware averaged $250,000, with about $85,000 for football. The largest group of schools had neither big-time football nor basketball programs and averaged less than $100,000 annually for their athletic expenditures (Koppett, 1971).

Ticket sales were found to account for nearly half of all the income earned from intercollegiate sport. Thus, waning attendance has posed a serious dilemma. All college athletic programs, big and small, need to generate ever *increasing* revenue to keep pace with accelerating costs. The dollar cost of athletics doubled between 1960 and 1970. So did revenue, but not in a balanced way. Data produced by the University of Missouri for the NCAA (and presented by Koppett, 1971) showed that income matched expenses only at schools with large-scale football programs; and expenditures were shown by this 1969 study to be increasing faster than income for colleges in general.

While big-time football seems to be the backbone of successful college athletic programs, it is not necessarily the panacea for fiscal woes that it appears to be. Football not only has the greatest potential for producing income, it is also much more expensive than any other sport. The cost of scholarships, coaching staffs, equipment, recruiting, physical facilities, travel, training tables, and promotion is far greater in football than in any other college sport and in many cases, than all other sports combined. After examining the results of a *Fortune* magazine survey of big-time college football conducted during the early 1960s, Myles Jackson (1962) concluded that college football had become a losing business. Both Koppett's article and one written for *Sports Illustrated* by Pat Ryan (1971) suggested that Jackson's conclusion is still valid today, probably even more so. Like Koppett, Ryan concluded that with the exception of those relatively few schools with financially successful big-time football programs, athletic austerity loomed ahead for the colleges.

MONEY, ORGANIZATION, AND THE MODERN ATHLETE

In *No Joy in Mudville*, Ralph Andreano (1965: 144) contended that the typical major leaguer "feels [a] direct and psychic association with the legendary players of the past; he is a part of American History and therefore above the din of the average guy who works for a weekly or hourly wage." In the mid-1960s, Charnofsky (1968) tried to test such assumptions concerning the self-conceptions of major league baseball players. He attempted to discover how the ball players viewed their occupation, and found that the modern ball players felt little connection with old-time baseball heroes and did not see themselves as being above the average working man. Although the players recognized their unusual athletic abilities, they saw themselves as similar to most other people in values, intelligence, and personality. To the ball players, money ranked in importance far above the fun, love, and challenge of the game and the prestige that could be earned from playing it. They believed that their occupation was an enjoyable but demanding business, with its share of undesirable features, such as spending a great deal of time away from home, traveling, and job insecurity.

This business-like atmosphere of sport is not for everyone. For example, Tom Meschery, in retiring from professional basketball after ten years as a player and just one year as a coach, said:

There was a time, and it was not so long ago, when things such as honor and loyalty were virtues in sport, and not objects of ridicule. It was a time when athletes drew pleasure and satisfaction from the essence of competition, not just from their paychecks. But somehow, with the introduction of big business, the concept of sports in this country has changed (1972: 56).

The transformation of professional sport into big business, in constant search of expanding markets and increased commercial gains, readily explains the shifting concern of professional athletes from the game itself to the financial security that can be achieved through it. It seems a logical development for these athletes to become increasingly business-like with their concern for bigger contracts, better fringe benefits, and pacing themselves to avoid unnecessary injuries or untimely fatigue as their bosses become calculating, profit motivated corporate executives. However, since the money in sport ultimately derives from fan interest, the commercial development of the sports industry and the professionalization of athletes may eventually undermine the success of both sports executives and athletes. For fans think of athletes as heroes, not money hungry, security motivated businessmen, and they like to see the game played with exciting abandon, heroically.

Thus, it appears that the modern professional athlete has been faced with a serious dilemma. Should he forsake the vast array of financial opportunities and concentrate mainly or exclusively on playing the game? Or, should he try to maximize financial rewards while they are still available—like people in other jobs normally do? Professional athletes feel that fans do not resent their affluence, but that they do resent the players' *apparent* greediness, lack of sincerity in endorsing products, lack of total concentration on the game, and their seeming willingness to put self-interest before the quality of the game and the enjoyment of those who support it—the spectators. However, these athletes also know that owners will try to pay them as little as possible and trade them or discard them arbitrarily in the interest of their own commercial gain. Furthermore, they know their athletic careers are short, that they could be ended prematurely by an injury at any time, and that their athletic skills, *per se,* are of little use in other occupational spheres. Apparently, today's professional athletes have generally decided to resolve this problem in favor of financial security.

Commercial opportunities have been pursued by amateur athletes as well. There is considerable evidence indicating that amateur skiers, tennis players, and track and field competitors have received payments and other material rewards from equipment manufacturers and veritable wages or salaries from public and private sources to support their amateur careers. In addition, amateur careers are frequently pursued in the hopes of earning professional contracts. One finds that high school baseball stars and talented college football and basketball players are often more concerned with demonstrating their individual skills for professional scouts than they are with making sacrifices for team success.

The unionlike organization of professional athletes (Scoville, 1974: 204–211) and their successful court battles (Rivkin, 1974) have enabled them to share an increased proportion of the current prosperity of professional sport and by such means, professional athletes have strengthened their individual and collective power and rights in their dealings with the professional sports establishment. Threatened boycotts like that which took place before the 1968 Mexico City Olympic Games have enabled amateur athletes also to alter the policies of the officials who rule their domain. How far such activities will go and where they will lead are not certain but it is likely that they will progress in accordance with the unresponsiveness of the managers of sport, that has been bred by bureaucratization and commercialization. It is likely that these processes and their effects upon the attitudes and behavior of those involved in sport will continue to reshape how the games are played.

It is easy to see how the commercially oriented approach of those who run sport has affected the very nature of sports contests. In an effort to attract more fans and to earn more money, the ruling hierarchy of sport has changed the basic structure of various games by extending the length of the seasons, instituting night contests, changing the dimensions and size of stadiums, introducing new playing surfaces, inventing exploding scoreboards, altering the uniforms worn by players, devising ingenious promotional stunts by players and nonplayers, and by making innumerable rule changes regarding how the game is played. Sports entrepreneurs have even created new sports, like the demolition derby and snowmobile racing.

SPORT AND TELEVISION

Gregory Stone (1955) discussed such changes in sport as reflecting a basic shift from pure play to spectacular display. Probably the dominant force encouraging this new orientation is television. Sports executives have dealt with the fear of the impact of television upon sport since the early 1950s by yielding to the television industry, dominant control over the form of sports events. Why have sports events started, paused, and ended on cue from TV directors? Why did soccer referee Peter Rhodes once wear an electronic beeper on his shoulder and signal an injury on cue to allow time for a one-minute commercial? Why do teams call time-outs at relatively inopportune stages in the game? Why has close pursuit of the passer been prohibited in football All-Star games? Why have athletes and coaches submitted to TV interviews during intensive preparation for important games and after agonizing defeats? Why has tennis sought to limit the length of matches through changes in its scoring system? Why have numerous other sports changes been made in the rules of play, the physical facilities, and the uniforms worn by players?

The basic justification for such concessions and modifications has been money, and most prominently, money from television contracts (see Johnson, 1969–70; Shecter, 1969: Ch. 2; Horowitz, 1974). While free newspaper publicity has significantly affected the commercial development of sport in America (Scott, 1971a: 161), and radio has helped make numerous sports popular, the commercial success of professional *and* big-time amateur sport in America depends more crucially *today* upon the television dollar. As William Ford of the Detroit Lions and the Ford Motor Company said, "There is no way we could survive without television. We couldn't make it without the income and we couldn't make it without the exposure" (cited in Durso, 1971: 255–256). It should be added that Ford is talking about the survival of a large-scale, highly commercialized industry, pro-football, which expanded between 1939 and 1969 from ten to twenty-six teams; from fifty-five to 182 league games per season; and from an estimated $150,000 to about $1 million for the average annual payroll per club (Durso, 1971: 120). One can be certain that his sentiments are shared by executives in other realms of the sports industry.

How much revenue does TV provide for the sports industry? In the U.S. in 1970, television had a commitment of over $60 million to college and professional football (Durso, 1971: 256). According to *Broadcasting* magazine, in 1973 radio and television rights to major league baseball reportedly cost over $40 million. A wide variety of professional and amateur sports organizations derive substantial earnings from television contracts. A quick glance through *TV Guide*'s sports listings for one week offers a clear indication of the extent sport has become dependent on television dollars.

If television were ever to withdraw its financial support from sport, the existing structure of highly professionalized, commercialized sport could very easily crumble. But why does television invest so many millions of dollars in the sports industry? And how well are they being compensated for their investment? CBS television sports director William MacPhail has offered a typical response to these questions for those in television:

> *Sports is a bad investment, generally speaking. The network needs it for prestige, for image, to satisfy the demands and desires of our affiliated stations. The rights have gotten so costly that we do sports as a public service rather than a profit-maker. We're doing great if we break even (cited in Durso, 1971: 264).*

Apparently, the television networks are currently locked into an especially frustrating competition with each other concerning the right to televise sports. Although the costs are becoming astronomical, not one of the networks is willing to drop out, for fear of losing prestige and advertising dollars. Thus, the bidding wars go on and the financial commitments earned by *winning* these wars continue to escalate. As the University of Notre Dame's athletic department tries to outdo that of the University of Southern California, the TV networks try to outdo each other by producing more spectacular and costly sports extravaganzas.

The sports industry's dependence on national and local network television for commercial success can be considered somewhat precarious. For this dependence is ultimately upon the willingness of businesses to pay increasing advertising costs during TV sports programs. One would expect that as soon as businesses begin to realize the decreasing returns from sponsoring TV sports shows, they would start putting their advertising dollars elsewhere. Even if sports programs continue to attract large (relatively affluent) audiences, a practical ceiling for their investment in sport is bound to be reached. Thus, larger sports audiences do not necessarily guarantee increased success for TV sports producers in the sale of commercial time during sports events. Smaller audiences almost guarantee *reduced* success in selling commercial time. If advertisers started withdrawing support from sports programming, then TV would eventually begin reducing its investment in sport, whether or not it results in a temporary loss of prestige. Where will all this business activity leave the sports industry? It may regain some of the control over sport it has lost to TV but it will also see its commercial fortunes spiral downward.

The history of professional boxing clearly indicates that the network television dollars which at one time provided a gold mine for sport can eventually cause its commercial decline. For the expanded television coverage which brings with it increased revenue can ultimately become overexposure. Just as business firms can become reluctant to make further investments in sport due to diminishing returns, fans can become bored with particular sports or sport in general.

In recent years, sports executives have become more aware of the dangers of too much live television coverage of their events, and the policy of "blacking-out" home games in many sports is one reflection of this awareness. However, before the 1973 professional football season, the United States Congress decided to limit the black-out policy to football games which were not sold out. Thus, an effort by professional football officials to maximize gate receipts, to maintain fan interest, and to preserve the financial success of their sport in the face of potentially threatening overexposure, was complicated by Congressional intervention. Particularly in view of this complication, which ironically, resulted from the tremendous popularity and success of professional football *and* threatens future financial growth, it will be interesting to see how sports executives balance their desire for television dollars against the possible dangers of oversaturation.

7 Sport and Social Change

Although it has been suggested that people performing sports roles of authority have been conservative and resisted change in sport, it should be obvious from our prior discussion that a variety of social processes (including commercialization and bureaucratization) have had a continuing, *dynamic* impact on the sports world. Changes in the rules, the roles, and the relationships in sport produced by social processes have occurred both subtly and dramatically, and these changes have happened despite the intentions and actions of sports authorities, and without the *conscious* assistance of them or anyone else involved in sport. In the remainder of this concluding chapter, the focus will be upon the distinctive structural causes, the character, and the likely social effects of some of the most basic reform and revolutionary movements in sport today. Thus, we will be considering deliberate and organized challenges to established sport.

THE VARIED FORMS
OF THE ATHLETIC "REVOLUTION"

During the early 1930s, practices of the American sports establishment, especially at the college level, were subjected to some scathing attacks. The major critics during this period were mostly from the ranks of middle-aged journalists, social reformers, and academicians. The main targets of criticism were: the corruption in recruiting, exorbitant financial expenditures, and drunken, riotous behavior in the college sports environment. Essentially, these criticisms were motivated by the belief that the institutional practices in sport did not foster the values and behavior that were *supposed* to be instilled through sports participation.

The dominant sports creed places emphasis on the importance of good character, self-discipline, respect for social control, and the enhancement of educational achievement through sport. There is no conclusive empirical proof that involvement in sports has actually done what the sports creed suggests it should do (Edwards, 1973: Ch. 10). Those critics who attacked established sport during the 1930s generally accepted the idealized conception and belief that sport should and could encourage the values and behavior emphasized in its dominant creed. Although there were a number of strongly antisport liberal educators (like Robert Maynard Hutchins), Edwards (1973: 351) argued that with few exceptions, the critics of this earlier era did not challenge the claimed potentialities of sport, nor did they propose radical alterations in its creed and basic institutional character. Thus, current attacks of the sports establishment may not be any more vitriolic than earlier ones, but they are more radical and more threatening to the dominant sports creed and the central institutional character of sport. Contemporary dissent has been widespread; the dissenters have been younger; many of them are presently or were formerly prominent athletes; and the attacks made of today's sports establishment have received more publicity than earlier criticisms.

The aristocratic, defensive, and self-serving attitudes and behavior of Olympic, NCAA, AAU, and professional sports officials, as well as the authoritarian perspective of many coaches, suggests an essentially conservative impulse of the authority structure of the modern institution of sport (Edwards, 1973: 91–92). Since the notion "institution" implies the persistence of socio-cultural patterns, it should not be surprising that guardians of the sport institution are the protectors of the *status quo*. In fact, the members of the sports establishment have been so resistant to change that they have reacted strongly to *any* organized or individual efforts to challenge the institutional character of sport. They have grouped together all apparently serious dissenters as equally disruptive influences upon the structure and functioning of sport. In addition, the ruling hierarchy has sought to discredit movements to transform sport or to disrupt its conventional practices by linking such behavior with subversive activities outside the sports arena. Thus, one finds ex-IOC President Avery Brundage publicly declaring in the wake of the 1972 tragedy in Munich, that the Olympics had been subjected to "two savage attacks," then he proceeded to equate the movement to remove the Rhodesian team from competition by virtue of its country's racist policies with the murder of the Israelis.

A social movement can be defined as a loosely organized collective attempt to reinterpret or transform one or more aspects of the patterned structural arrangements or cultural emphases in a society. Social movements can be distinguished in a number of ways. For example, there may be distinctions between the social sources, the nature of supporters, and the basic aims of different social movements. Thus, there are a number of distinct social movements in sport today. In the ensuing discussion, four movements will be distinguished on the basis of their characteristic social sources, supporters, and aims. They will be called respectively: conventional labor activism; egalitarian activism; "shamateur" activism; and democratic activism. It is assumed that the first three movements are essentially "reformist" in character because they are *generally* aimed at reshaping institutional rules or practices, but not the basic institutional character of sport. The fourth movement is much more radical or "revolutionary" in character because it is aimed at transforming the basic institutional nature of sport—its predominant emphases on achievement or winning, spectator welfare, money, and large-scale, bureaucratic organization.

Conventional labor activism in sport has derived mainly from the monopolistic practices of professional sports club owners and their economic exploitation of the athletes contractually bound to them. It includes threatened and actual player strikes, boycotts, and the pursuit of collective bargaining through full time, professional bargaining agents and unionlike player representatives. This social movement has been paralleled on an individual level by legal cases against professional sports and the owners like the suits by Curt Flood (1970) brought against baseball's reserve clause; by Connie Hawkins against the National Basketball Association (NBA) for excluding him from league play due to his alleged involvement in the basketball scandal of the early 1960s; and by Spencer Haywood challenging the "four-year college rule" maintained by the NBA and other professional leagues and sports. It has also been paralleled by the increasing representation of athletes by professional agents during individual contract negotiations, by the occurrence of arbitration hearings, and by the prevalence of "holdouts."

Conventional labor activism has been a phenomenon of professional sport. It has been the most militant where the owners have been especially conservative and unresponsive and where the player's associations have been the strongest. Thus, the most militant unionlike activity has occurred recently in professional baseball, football, and basketball in America. Significantly, this has been a movement uniting disgruntled players of different races and social backgrounds. Like labor activism in general, the labor movement in sport has been aimed primarily at increasing salaries and fringe benefits, improving working conditions, and enhancing the job and financial security of the workers—i.e. the athletes.

The egalitarian movement in sport has also frequently been oriented toward the distribution of rewards. However, there is a fundamental difference between the economic focus of egalitarian activism and the general economic orientation of conventional labor activism in sport. While the labor movement has sought to improve the economic status of professional athletes, the egalitarian movement has been aimed at improving the economic, political, and social status of *black* athletes. The egalitarian movement has been prompted by the institutional practice of racial discrimination in sport which was previously discussed.

Perhaps the most prominent figure in the egalitarian movement has been

Harry Edwards. His efforts to increase pride and intolerance of racial discrimination among black athletes have directly or indirectly resulted in victory stand demonstrations against exploitation of American black athletes. At the Summer Olympics, threatened boycotts forced the ouster from Olympic competition of South Africa in 1968 and Rhodesia in 1972, by reason of their apartheid policies. The influence of Edwards and other leaders of the egalitarian movement may also be seen in the wave of threatened and actual boycotts of college sports by black athletes in response to the alleged discriminatory practices by schools, coaches, and other athletic administrators. Symbolic of the thrust of this movement is the Olympic Project for Human Rights organized by Edwards before the 1968 Olympic Games (see Edwards, 1969, *The Revolt of the Black Athlete*).

Edwards has described the primary supporters of the egalitarian movement as black people who are typically middle class in orientation (if not in fact), educated, and active or former college or professional athletes. He has asserted that the basic aim of this movement is equal opportunity for blacks in sport—in particular, a reliance on achievement, rather than race, as the basis for decisions about participation, financial compensation, and the occupancy of positions of control. Thus, the egalitarian movement is not aimed at altering the basic institutional character of sport any more than the labor movement, but it *is* aimed at a significant restructuring of sport's stratification system with respect to race. Black activists interested in seeing the perpetuation and growth of the current prosperity of sport are demanding that more prosperity reach black hands and that more of the key decisions about the functioning of sport be made by black minds.

Shamateur activism is a reform movement of former Olympic athletes. It is a response to the aristocratic exclusiveness of the rules of eligibility for Olympic competition, its resultant hypocrisy, and the personal guilt felt by "shamateur" athletes. This hypocrisy and guilt have been nurtured by an inconsistent, seemingly arbitrary, enforcement of the eligibility rules and by the veneer of amateurism maintained by athletes who must accept financial support to sustain their involvement. The shamateur movement has been spearheaded by the World Sports Foundation (WSF), which was founded in 1972 by Suzy Chaffee, a member of the 1968 U.S. Ski Team, and Jack Kelly, a former Olympian and the president of the Amateur Athletic Union of the United States (AAU). Before the 1972 Munich Olympics, a petition was sent to competing athletes outlining the basic objectives of the shamateur movement (see Lyman, 1972: 8):

1. The individual athlete must have the right to determine the extent of training time required instead of the present sixty-day limit.
2. The National Olympic Committees and sports associations shall be responsible for arranging for athletes to be paid expense money, broken time payments and insurance coverage in connection with training and competition, whether these sources be private, governmental, or commercial.

3. Athletes may receive scholarships and financial assistance while fulfilling educational requirements, and may receive remuneration for actual employment in the athlete's sport, including positions as coaches.
4. Athletes may accept remuneration for television and other public appearances not involving actual competition in the athlete's sport. Remuneration for endorsements of commercial products connected with the athlete's sport may be accepted, but a share of such remuneration is subject to the rules of the International Federations and must be given to National Associations and other participating athletes.
5. National and International Federations and Olympic organizations shall be required to have competing or recently retired athletes as voting and fully participating members of such bodies.

These objectives do not seem to challenge the basic institutional character of sport. Indeed, the concern with making the payment of amateur athletes more open appears to reinforce the commercial orientation of sport. Only the goal of granting increased control over operation of the Olympics to participants implicitly suggests an orientation that runs counter to the current conception of sport as an enterprise controlled by aristocrats primarily concerned with the tastes of the paying customers, the public, or the elite.

If we did not know as much as we do about the big business of *amateur* sport, this more democratic, participant orientation would seem quite natural in the amateur context. However, since the structural distinctions between amateur and professional sport are more a matter of scale than substance, the idea of having the Olympics run by the athletes almost seems radical. This idea is clearly articulated by Suzy Chaffee's (1972) report of WSF activities in Munich, which she wrote shortly after her return from the 1972 Games: "The Games should be for the participants and not the ruling aristocracy, the commercial magnates or the political commissars. The WSF believes that the rules must change to reflect a return of the Games to the athletes." The desire to recapture the pure amateur ideal with respect to the control of sport makes the thrust of shamateur activism somewhat more radical than the other reform movements discussed. However, it is the integration of this aim with a number of other equally radical ones that makes the democratic movement revolutionary.

The democratic movement in sport can be viewed as a reaction to the all-consuming passion for winning at any cost and to the dehumanization of athletes and athletic performances. Both of these presumed patterns in sport are seen as consequences of the authoritarianism of coaches and others in formal positions of authority. The substance of democratic activism is best illustrated by the ideas and activities of Jack Scott (1971a), cofounder of the Institute for the Study of Sport and Society, and former Chairman of the Department of Physical Education and Intercollegiate Athletics at Oberlin College. Scott has been committed to articulating and realizing the ideals of what Edwards has called the "humanitarian counter-creed."

According to Edwards (1973: 336–341), the humanitarian values of the democratic movement have been accepted mainly by white, educated, middle-class young people either affiliated with universities or active (at some time) in professional sport. The reason this movement has been called "democratic" here is its central belief that athletics should be *of* the people (participants), *for* the pleasure of the people (participants), and run *by* the people (participants). Its ideology has been called "humanitarian" because of the concern of its members for the welfare of fellow competitors. Scott has envisioned the sports arena as a place where individuals can pursue excellence through maximum exertion of their physical skills *and* where successful athletic competitors help less-successful athletes achieve their potential. This ideology is classified as humanitarian for the added reason that emphasis on the violent destruction of one's opponent is strongly opposed. In this context, it is little wonder that Scott has been perceived and labeled by the sports establishment as a dangerous radical—even before his name was linked with the Patty Hearst case. However, Scott views himself as an unabashed "jock." What he detests most about sport are its excessive commercialism and pressure to win that breed authoritarianism; the drug-taking, the recruiting violations and brutality; its elitist, spectator orientation; its excessive concern with proving masculinity and denying females a chance to participate; and the general conservative characteristics. These are precisely what the establishment of sport feels compelled to preserve (see Brown, 1972). Thus, the deep rooted, extreme antagonism between the democratic activists and the defenders of the sport institution is easy to understand.

To varying degrees, the labor, the egalitarian, the shamateur, and the democratic movements all challenge the present structure of sport. However, it is not immediately apparent how they will change its institutional character. The first two movements are oriented toward changing the patterned distribution of rewards in sport. Nevertheless, while labor and egalitarian activism will improve the status of professional and black athletes in the short run, they may also contribute to the commercial *decline* of sport in the long run. For in demanding increased financial security, the labor movement is also demanding the continued commercial expansion of sport. But fan interest may drop from oversaturation and disillusionment or disgruntlement with player militance, and television investment may decrease as a result of the loss of fans and advertising.

As for the egalitarian movement, Edwards (1973: 342) proposed that its success in changing the economic reward structure and control hierarchy of sport may ultimately mean a precipitous decline of interest if white fans are not able to identify with an essentially black sports world. Without the financial support of white fans, the white dominated mass media and business establishment, the overwhelming success of black egalitarian activists in sport would be a shallow victory. Thus, continued and increasing pressure from labor and egalitarian activists may unintentionally transform the basic institutional character of sport into something quite different from what they desire.

The partial success of the shamateur movement is likely to bring about, (1) a liberalization of the amateur or Olympic eligibility criteria; (2) expanded opportunities for participation by athletes of less privileged status; (3) decreased hypocrisy and guilt about the acceptance of financial compensation; and (4) greater responsiveness by amateur officials to the needs of athletes whom they are supposed to serve. The representation of athletes on the U.S. Olympic Committee, the appointment of a member of the 1972 Olympic team to the vice-presidency of the U.S. Ski Association, and the apparent willingness of IOC President Lord Killanin to rid amateur sport of some of its inequities are evidence of limited success in its initial effort to reform amateur sport. Yet the continued success of this shamateur movement could lead to unintended, undesired effects.

Although athletes may assume increasing control over the amateur sports realm, their concern for fellow athletes needing financial backing could eventually transform amateur sport into a highly commercial enterprise. Even without direct financial compensation for competition, the legitimate pursuit of a variety of commercial ventures tied to sports involvement may lead to a greater dedication to these business interests than to the athletic performance that spawned them. A more liberal policy concerning commercialism could eventually mean the demand of guaranteed expense money or even small salaries for a vast number of athletes and of course, if this were to happen, there would be little practical difference between amateur and professional sports *and* the problems facing both. Indeed, increasing commercialization of amateur sport could bring about the decline of *both* high-level amateur and professional sport.

Harry Edwards (1973: 341) argued that Jack Scott's athletic revolution is not likely to be very successful because the sport institution's emphases upon such values as winning at any cost, commercial success, and competitiveness are the dominant values of American society. This sharing of cultural emphases between sport and society reinforces the fans' respect for the traditional values and institutional practices, and reinforces traditional relationships between coaches and athletes. Edwards' contention would seem valid insofar as the cultural themes of American society that are related to sport do not change. But, *if* the moral values of the youth counterculture have a significant impact on the young people of American society, one can expect a gradual shift in the values and institutional character of sport; for increasing value discrepancies between sport and society place increasing pressure on sport *as an institution* to change in accordance with societal change. If democratic activists are in tune with societal changes, then one would anticipate their chances for success to be enhanced. Of course, it is crucial to reiterate that success for democratic activists means the decline of sport as we know it today and the growth of a more amateur, participant oriented, and participant run form of sport pursued for pleasure, rather than for profit.

Parenthetically, the activities of the labor, egalitarian, and shamateur movements may ultimately and unintentionally contribute to the basic changes in sport desired by Scott.

The final irony of the expansion of modern sport may be that the very forces of bureaucratization, commercialization, and professionalization marking this growth, may in turn be primarily responsible for its decline. It is not clear where the corporate development of sport will lead or how sports reformers or revolutionaries will affect this development. However, one intriguing possibility is that there will be a gradual decay of commercialized, professionalized, spectator oriented, large-scale sport and a rebirth of play-like amateurism.

References

Andreano, Ralph
1965   No Joy in Mudville. Cambridge, Mass.: Schenkman.
Annarino, Anthony A.
1953   "The contributions of athletics to social mobility." Paper presented at the Annual Proceedings of the College Physical Education Association. New York.
Beisser, Arnold R.
1967   The Madness in Sports. New York: Appleton-Century-Crofts.
Bend, Emil
1968   "The impact of athletic participation on academic and career aspiration and achievement." New Brunswick, N.J.: The National Football Foundation and Hall of Fame.
Blalock, Hubert M.
1962   "Occupational discrimination: some theoretical propositions." Social Problems 9:240–247.
Bouton, Jim
1970   Ball Four. New York: World.
Brown, Gwilym S.
1972   "Jeepers! Peepers is in charge now." Sports Illustrated (October 23).
Buhrmann, Hans G.
1972   "Scholarship and athletics in junior high school." International Review of Sport Sociology 7:119–128.
Cady, Steve
1972   "A study finds cheating abounds in sport." The New York Times (December 11).
Caillois, Roger
1961   Man, Play, and Games (translated by Meyer Barash). New York: Free Press.
Chaffee, Suzy
1972   "Report on World Sports Foundation activities in Munich." (October 5) New York: World Sports Foundation.
Charnofsky, Harold
1968   "The major league professional baseball player: self-conceptions versus the popular image." International Review of Sport Sociology 3:39–53.

Coleman, James S.
1961   The Adolescent Society. New York: Free Press.
Durso, Joseph
1971   The All-American Dollar: The Big Business of Sports. Boston: Houghton Mifflin.
Edwards, Harry
1969   The Revolt of the Black Athlete. New York: Free Press.
1973   Sociology of Sport. Homewood, III.: Dorsey.
Eggleston, John
1965   "Secondary schools and Oxbridge Blues." British Journal of Sociology 16:232–242.
Eitzen, D. Stanley
1970   "The effect of group structure on the success of athletic teams." Paper presented at the Seventh World Congress of Sociology. Varna, Bulgaria.
and N. Yetman
1972   "Managerial succession, longevity, and organizational effectiveness." Administrative Science Quarterly 7:110–116.
Essing, W.
1970   "Team line-up and team achievement in European football." In Contemporary Psychology of Sport, edited by Gerald S. Kenyon. Chicago: Athletic Institute.
Festinger, Leon
1950   "Informal social communication." Psychological Review 57:271–282.
Fiedler, Fred E.
1954   "Assumed similarity measures as predictors of team effectiveness." Journal of Abnormal and Social Psychology 49:381–388.
1960   "The leader's psychological distance and group effectiveness." In Group Dynamics, edited by O. Cartwright and A. Zander. Evanston, III.: Row, Peterson.
Fimrite, Ron
1971   "We expect them to storm the gates." Sports Illustrated (September 6).
Flood, Curt
1970   The Way It Is. New York: Trident.
Furst, R. Terry
1971   "Social change and the commercialization of professional sports." International Review of Sport Sociology 6:153–170.
Gamson, William A. and Norman A. Scotch
1964   "Scapegoating in baseball." American Journal of Sociology 70:69–72.
Gilbert, Bill
1969   "Three-part series on drugs in sport." Sports Illustrated (June 23, 30; July 7).
and Nancy Williamson
1973   "Three-part series on women in sport." Sports Illustrated (May 28; June 4, 11).
Grusky, Oscar
1963a   "Managerial succession and organizational effectiveness." American Journal of Sociology 69:21–31.
1963b   "The effects of formal structure on managerial recruitment: a study of baseball organization." Sociometry 26:345–363.
1964   "Reply to Gamson and Scotch." American Journal of Sociology 70:72–73.
Harres, Bea
1968   "Attitudes of students toward women's athletic competition." Research Quarterly 39:278–284.
Hart, Marie
1971   "Sport: women sit in the back of the bus." Psychology Today (October): 64–66.
Hoch, Paul
1972   Rip Off the Big Game. Garden City, N.Y.: Doubleday-Anchor.

Hodges, Harold M.
1964   Social Stratification. Cambridge, Mass.: Schenkman.
Horowitz, Ira
1974   "Sports broadcasting." In Government and the Sports Business, edited by Roger G. Noll. Washington, D.C.: Brookings Institution.
Huizinga, Johan
1938   Homo Ludens. Boston: Beacon.
Jackson, Myles
1962   "College football has become a losing business." Fortune (December).
Johnson, William
1969–70   "Five-part series on television and sports." Sports Illustrated (December 22, 1969; January 5, 12, 19, 26, 1970).
Kenyon, Gerald S.
1969a   "Explaining sport involvement." Paper presented at the Fall Conference of the Eastern Association for Physical Education of College Women. Lake Placid, New York.
1969b   "Sport involvement: a conceptual go and some consequences thereof." In Sociology of Sport, edited by Gerald S. Kenyon. Chicago: Athletic Institute.
Klein, Michael and Gerd Christiansen
1969   "Group composition, group structure, and group effectiveness of basketball teams." In Sport, Culture, and Society, edited by John W. Loy and Gerald S. Kenyon. New York: Macmillan.
Koppett, Leonard
1971   "Colleges question old views on sports." The New York Times (January 11).
Landers, Daniel M. and Gunther Luschen
1974   "Team performance outcome and the cohesiveness of competitive coacting groups." International Review of Sport Sociology 2(9):57–69.
Lenk, Hans
1969   "Top performance despite internal conflict." In Sport, Culture, and Society, edited by John W. Loy and Gerald S. Kenyon. New York: Macmillan.
Lever, Janet
1972   "Soccer as a Brazilian way of life." In Games Sport and Power, edited by Gregory Stone. New Brunswick, N.J.: Transaction.
Litchfield, Edward H. with Myron Cope
1962   "Saturday's hero is doing fine." Sports Illustrated (July 8).
Loy, John W.
1969a   "The study of sport and social mobility." In Sociology of Sport, edited by Gerald S. Kenyon. Chicago: Athletic Institute.
1969b   "The nature of sport: a definitional effort." In Sport, Culture, and Society, edited by John W. Loy and Gerald S. Kenyon. New York: Macmillan.
1972   "Social origins and occupational mobility patterns of a selected sample of American athletes." International Review of Sport Sociology 7:5–23.
  and Joseph F. McElvogue
1970   "Racial segregation in American sport." International Review of Sport Sociology 5:5–23.
  and George H. Sage
1972   "Social origins, academic achievement, athletic achievement, and career mobility patterns of college coaches." Paper presented at the Annual Meeting of the American Sociological Association. New Orleans, Louisiana.
Luschen, Gunther
1969   "Social stratification and social mobility among young sportsmen." In Sport, Culture, and Society, edited by John W. Loy and Gerald S. Kenyon. New York: Macmillan.
Lyman, David H.
1972   "The future of the Olympics." The Student Skier Three (Holiday 8–9).

Mandell, Richard
1971   The Nazi Olympics. New York: Macmillan.
Martens, Rainer and James Peterson
1971   "Group cohesiveness as a determinant of success and member satisfaction in team performance." International Review of Sport Sociology 6:49–59.
McGrath, Joseph E.
1962   "The influence of positive interpersonal relations on adjustment effectiveness in rifle teams." Journal of Abnormal and Social Psychology 65:365–375.
McIntosh, Peter
1971   Sport in Society. London: Watts.
McIntyre, Thomas D.
1970   "A field experimental study of attitude change in four biracial small groups." Unpublished doctoral dissertation. Pennsylvania State University.
Meggyesy, Dave
1970   Out of Their League. Berkeley: Ramparts.
Melnick, Merrill J. and Martin M. Chemers
1974   "Effects of group social structure on the success of basketball teams." Research Quarterly 45:1–8.
Meschery, Tom
1972   "There is a disease in sports now . . ." Sports Illustrated (October 2).
Metheny, Eleanor
1970   "Symbolic forms of movement: the feminine image in sports." In Sport and American Society, edited by George H. Sage. Reading, Mass.: Addison-Wesley.
Meyer, Herbert H.
1951   "Factors related to success in the human relations aspect of work-group leadership." Psychological Monographs 65:1–29.
Myers, Albert
1962   "Team competition, success, and the adjustment of group members." Journal of Abnormal and Social Psychology 65:325–332.
Ogilvie, Bruce C. and Thomas A. Tutko
1971   "Sport: if you want to build character, try something else." Psychology Today (October):60–63.
Oliver, Chip
1971   High for the Game. New York: William Morrow.
Olmsted, Michael S.
1959   The Small Group. New York: Random House.
Page, Charles H.
1973   "The world of sport and its study." In Sport and Society: An Anthology, edited by John T. Talamini and Charles H. Page. Boston: Little, Brown.
Parrish, Bernie
1971   They Call It a Game. New York: Dial.
Pooley, John
1968   "Ethnic soccer clubs in Milwaukee: a study in assimilation." M.S. thesis: University of Wisconsin.
Rehberg, Richard and Walter E. Schafer
1968   "Participation in interscholastic athletics and college expectations." American Journal of Sociology 63:732–740.
Richardson, Deane E.
1962   "Ethical conduct in sport situations." National College Physical Education Association for Men—Proceedings 66:98–104.
Riesman, David and Reuel Denney
1951   "Football in America: a study in culture diffusion." American Quarterly 3:309–319.

Rivkin, Steven R.
1974   "Sports leagues and the federal antitrust laws." In Government and the Sports Business, edited by Roger G. Noll. Washington, D.C.: Brookings Institution.

Russell, Bill
1966   Go Up for Glory. New York: Coward, McCann.

Ryan, Pat
1971   "A grim run to fiscal daylight." Sports Illustrated (February 1).

Sage, John N.
1967   "Adolescent values and the non-participating college athlete." Paper presented at the Convention of the Southern Section of the Canadian Association of Health, Physical Education, and Recreation. San Fernando, California.

Schafer, Walter E.
1968   "Athletic success and social mobility." Paper presented at the Annual Meeting of the American Association of Health, Physical Education, and Recreation. St. Louis, Missouri.
1969   "Some social sources and consequences of interscholastic athletics: the case of participation and delinquency." International Review of Sport Sociology 4:63–79.
1971   "Sport and youth counterculture: contrasting socialization themes." Paper presented at the Conference on Sport and Social Deviancy. Brockport, New York.

   and J. Michael Armer
1968   "Athletes are not inferior students." Trans-action (November):21–26,61–62.
1972   "On scholarship and interscholastic athletics." In Sport: Readings From a Sociological Perspective, edited by Eric Dunning. Toronto: University of Toronto Press.

   and Richard Rehberg
1970   "Athletic participation, college aspirations, and college encouragement." Pacific Sociological Review 13:182–186.

Scott, Jack
1971a   The Athletic Revolution. New York: Free Press.
1971b   "It's not how you play the game, but what pill you take." The New York Times (October 17).

Scoville, James G.
1974   "Labor relations in sports." In Government and the Sports Business, edited by Roger G. Noll. Washington, D.C.: Brookings Institution.

Shaw, Gary
1972   Meat on the Hoof. New York: St. Martin's.

Shecter, Leonard
1969   The Jocks. Indianapolis: Bobbs-Merrill.

Smelser, Neil J.
1962   The Theory of Collective Behavior. New York: Free Press.

Snyder, Eldon E.
1969   "A longitudinal analysis of the relationship between high school student values, social participation and educational-occupational achievement." Sociology of Education 42:261–270.
1971   "Athletic dressing room slogans as folklore: a means of socialization." Paper presented at the Annual Meeting of the American Sociological Association. Denver, Colorado.

Spady, William G.
1970   "Lament for the letterman: effects of peer status and extracurricular activities on goals and achievement." American Journal of Sociology 75:680–702.

Spreitzer, Elmer and Meredith Pugh
1973   "Interscholastic athletics and educational expectations." Sociology of Education 46:171–182.

Stogdill, Ralph M.
1963   "Team achievement under high motivation." Business Research Monograph. Ohio State University Press.

Stone, Gregory P.
1955   "American sports: play and display." Chicago Review 9:83–100.

Stone, Gregory P. (ed.)
1972   Games, Sport and Power. New Brunswick, N.J.: Transaction.

Sutton, Francis X. et al.
1956   The American Business Creed. Cambridge, Mass.: Harvard University Press.

Talamini, John T. and Charles H. Page (eds.)
1973   Sport and Society: An Anthology. Boston: Little, Brown.

Taylor, Ian
1971   "Soccer consciousness and soccer hooliganism." In Images of Deviance, edited by Stanley Cohen. Middlesex, England: Penguin.

1972   " 'Football mad': a speculative sociology of football hooliganism." In Sport: Readings From a Sociological Perspective, edited by Eric Dunning. Toronto: University of Toronto Press.

Underwood, John
1969   "Three-part series on the desperate coach." Sports Illustrated (August 25; September 1, 8).

Veblen, Thorstein
1899   Theory of the Leisure Class. New York: Macmillan.

Velt, Hans
1970   "Some remarks upon the elementary interpersonal relations within ball game teams." In Contemporary Psychology of Sport, edited by Gerald S. Kenyon. Chicago: Athletic Institute.

Vos, Koos, and Brinkman W.
1967   "Succes en cohesie in sportgroepen" (Success and cohesion in sports). Sociologische Gios 14:30–40.

Webb, Harry
1968a   "Success patterns of college athletes." Paper presented at the National Convention of the American Association of Health, Physical Education, and Recreation. St. Louis, Missouri.

1968b   "Social backgrounds of college athletes." Paper presented at the National Convention of the American Association of Health, Physical Education, and Recreation. St. Louis, Missouri.

1969a   "Professionalization of attitudes toward play among adolescents." In Sociology of Sport, edited by Gerald S. Kenyon. Chicago: Athletic Institute.

1969b   "Reaction to Loy paper." In Sociology of Sport, edited by Gerald S. Kenyon. Chicago: Athletic Institute.

Weinberg, S. Kirson and Henry Arond
1952   "The occupational culture of the boxer." American Journal of Sociology 57:460–469.

Wolf, David
1972   Foul! New York: Holt, Rinehart, and Winston.

Yetman, Norman R. and D. Stanley Eitzen
1971   "Black athletes on intercollegiate basketball teams: an empirical test of discrimination." In Majority and Minority, edited by Norman R. Yetman and C. Hoy Steele. Boston: Allyn and Bacon.

Zurcher, Louis and Arnold Meadow
1972   "On bullfights and baseball: an example of interaction of social institutions." In Sport: Readings From a Sociological Perspective, edited by Eric Dunning. Toronto: University of Toronto Press.

THE BOBBS-MERRILL REPRINT SERIES

The author recommends for supplementary reading the following related materials. Please fill out this form and mail.

Indicate the number of reprints desired.

____ **Bendix, Reinhard.** "Bureaucracy: The Problem and Its Setting." American Sociological Review, 1947, pp. 493–507.   **S–16**/66425   60¢

____ **Clark, Burton R. and Martin Trow.** "Determinants of the Sub-Cultures of College Students: The Organizational Context." College Peer Groups, edited by Theodore M. Newcomb and Everett K. Wilson. Aldine Publishing Company, 1967, pp. 17–70 plus bibliography.
                                            S–559/66936 $1.20

____ **Coleman, James S.** "The Adolescent Subculture and Academic Achievement." American Journal of Sociology, 1960, pp. 337–347.
                                            S–361/66739   60¢

____ **Davis, Kingsley and Wilbert E. Moore.** "Some Principles of Stratification." American Sociological Review, 1945, pp. 242–249; bound with: Melvin M. Tumin, "Some Principles of Stratification: A Critical Analysis." American Sociological Review, 1953, pp. 387–394; and Kingsley Davis and Wilbert E. Moore, "Reply" and "Comment" Ibid. pp. 394–397.
                                            S–68/66474   60¢

____ **Dentler, Robert A. and Kai T. Erikson.** "The Functions of Deviance in Groups." Social Problems, 1959, pp. 98–107.   **S–71**/66477   60¢

____ **Flacks, Richard.** "The Liberated Generation: An Exploration of the Roots of Student Protest." Journal of Social Issues, 1967, pp. 52–75.
                                            S–690/68708   80¢

____ **Lieberson, Stanley and Glenn V. Fuguitt.** "Negro-White Occupational Differences in the Absence of Discrimination." American Journal of Sociology, 1967, pp. 188–200.   **S–724**/68741   60¢

____ **McClelland, David C.** "Some Social Consequences of Achievement Motivation." Nebraska Symposium on Motivation, edited by M. R. Jones. University of Nebraska Press, 1955, pp. 41–65.
                                            S–457/66835   80¢

____ **Pettigrew, Thomas F.** "Complexity and Change in American Racial Patterns: A Social Psychological View." Daedalus, 1965, pp. 974–1008.
                                            S–613/66990   80¢

____ **Rainwater, Lee.** "Crucible of Identity: The Negro Lower-Class Family." Daedalus, 1966, pp. 172–216.   **BC–234**/67614 $1.00

____ **Rossi, Alice S.** "Equality Between the Sexes: An Immodest Proposal." Daedalus, 1964, pp. 607–652.   **S–750**/68767 $1.00

____ **Selznick, Philip.** "Foundations of the Theory of Organization." American Sociological Review, 1948, pp. 25–35.   **S–255**/66646   60¢

—— **Siegel, Paul M.** "On the Cost of Being a Negro." Sociological Inquiry, 1965, pp. 41–57. **S–761**–68778 60¢

—— **Warner, W. Lloyd.** "What Social Class is in America." Social Class in America, edited by Warner, Marchia Meeker, and Kenneth Eells. Science Research Associates, Inc., 1949, Chapter One, pp. 3–33. **S–302**/66681 80¢

—— **Wrong, Dennis H.** "The Functional Theory of Stratification: Some Neglected Considerations." American Sociological Review, 1959, pp. 772–782. **S–322**/66701 60¢

The Bobbs-Merrill Company, Inc.
Continuing Education and
College Department
4300 West 62nd Street
Indianapolis, Indiana 46268

Instructors ordering for class use will receive *upon request* a complimentary desk copy of each title ordered in quantities of 10 or more. Refer to author and *complete* letter-number code when ordering reprints.

☐ Payment enclosed   ☐ Bill me (on orders for $5 or more only)

_____ Course number   _____ Expected enrollment

☐ For examination   ☐ Desk copy

Bill To_____

ADDRESS_____

CITY_____ STATE_____ ZIP_____

Ship To_____

ADDRESS_____

CITY_____ STATE_____ ZIP_____

Please send me _____ copies of the sociology reprints catalog.

Please send me related reprints catalogs in_____

_____

Any reseller is free to charge whatever price he wishes for our books.

For your convenience please use complete form when placing your order.